The Answer Is Spiritual

The Answer Is Spiritual

A Collection of Scriptural Lessons for Daily Living

DAVID MUSGRAVE

Foreword by John Board

RESOURCE *Publications* · Eugene, Oregon

THE ANSWER IS SPIRITUAL
A Collection of Scriptural Lessons for Daily Living

Copyright © 2024 David Musgrave. All rights reserved. Except for brief quotations in critical publications or reviews, no part of this book may be reproduced in any manner without prior written permission from the publisher. Write: Permissions, Wipf and Stock Publishers, 199 W. 8th Ave., Suite 3, Eugene, OR 97401.

Resource Publications
An Imprint of Wipf and Stock Publishers
199 W. 8th Ave., Suite 3
Eugene, OR 97401

www.wipfandstock.com

PAPERBACK ISBN: 978-1-6667-8436-7
HARDCOVER ISBN: 978-1-6667-8437-4
EBOOK ISBN: 978-1-6667-8438-1

VERSION NUMBER 12/29/23

Unless otherwise noted, all Old Testament translations are those of the author.

Scriptures marked ASV are taken from the AMERICAN STANDARD VERSION (ASV), public domain.

All New Testament translations, unless otherwise noted, are from The ESV® Bible (The Holy Bible, English Standard Version®), © 2001 by Crossway, a publishing ministry of Good News Publishers. Used by permission. All rights reserved.

Scripture quotations marked RSV are from the Revised Standard Version of the Bible, copyright © 1946, 1952, and 1971 National Council of the Churches of Christ in the United States of America. Used by permission. All rights reserved worldwide.

Contents

Foreword by John Board | vii
Acknowledgments | ix
Introduction | xi

January | 1
February | 32
March | 61
April | 92
May | 122
June | 153
July | 183
August | 214
September | 245
October | 275
November | 306
December | 336

Afterword | 367
Index | 369

Foreword

When the Covid-19 pandemic hit the world in 2020, many teachers of God's word sought to reach a "captive" audience to help them cope with something this generation had never experienced. I began recording a daily weekday video devotional for a congregation. Soon members requested adding other family and friends to the group who received the daily weekday videos. In a matter of weeks, I began receiving a daily weekday devotional email from an instructor. I thought to myself, "Here is another way to provide spiritual food for a world searching for answers." I also thought, "This may be such a time of pause that people would take time to read these valuable thoughts regarding God's revelation to humanity."

I first met Dr. David Musgrave while a student in one of his many language classes in pursuit of my degree in biblical studies. Very quickly, I learned that Dr. Musgrave was a humble man. It was clear he was a scholar, yet there was something quite different in his approach to his teaching—or, more correctly stated, in his approach to his students. Under his instruction, I felt Dr. Musgrave had a strong desire to aid his students in understanding the language, whether Hebrew, Sumerian, or Akkadian. He had a unique skill that made me feel like we were in this pursuit of knowledge together as a team.

Dr. Musgrave utilized this same unique skill in his weekday devotional emails entitled "Dave's Daily." As I read the emails, I again felt I was involved in the quest with Dr. Musgrave. This time the pursuit was a greater understanding and application of Scripture. After several weeks of reading "Dave's Daily," I asked Dr. Musgrave if he had plans to publish these emails in a book. The value of his wisdom and understanding of Scripture could serve to bless not only those living today but all those who would read them in generations to come. There is value in publishing these electronic messages in a paper form.

The strength of "Dave's Daily" lies in the fact that Dr. Musgrave has taken his deep knowledge of Scripture and has related it to all readers. It is easy to understand, yet each day contains a thought of great depth for the advanced student of Scripture. Dr. Musgrave also utilizes the principle of allowing Scripture to interpret Scripture.

Dr. Musgrave does not seek to provide fluff that might excite the mind but provide little lasting value. Rather, he uses his skill set as a student of words to convey each thought carefully. When commenting on God's revelation to humanity, the reader should expect such a high standard. It will provide lasting value for generations to come.

John Board
Elizabethtown Church of Christ
Elizabethtown, Kentucky

Acknowledgments

I WOULD LIKE HEREIN to gratefully acknowledge the assistance of Derrick Allen for invaluable lexical help, for encouragement through feedback, and for being a great student; John Board, for his encouraging words regarding these lessons, his literary contribution herein, as well as his longstanding friendship; Mark Phillips for his friendship and feedback regarding these lessons; Kip Ping for his support, encouragement, friendship, and our work as fellow elders; all of my readers for reading these lessons, not to mention the many words of encouragement in response hereto (the most positive feedback I've ever received in anything related to ministry); Ann, my beloved wife of forty years, whose contributions to this work, and to me as a work in progress, go beyond saying. With love and appreciation to all.

Introduction

I PERSONALLY BELIEVE THAT there are no easy answers to most of life's problems, and there certainly isn't one answer that can solve all of life's problems. The title of this book is offered to reinforce to all of us the need to incorporate a spiritual mindset in our daily lives, and, perhaps especially, to do so with regard to our approach to problems. To do this can serve the purpose of contributing to our own spiritual growth, to help us gain strength to carry on in this life, and to help us by the life we live ultimately to glorify God.

As noted in the foreword, this work came about right after the start of the lockdown of 2020, as a daily email lesson entitled "Dave's Daily." The title was based on the fact that the congregation where I serve as an elder, Loveland Heights Church of Christ, primarily address me with the casual "Dave." The reader can probably tell that some of the lessons reflect the life context of the lockdown.

One of my primary goals in this effort is to help all of us to adopt a spiritual mindset to life, especially one that is conditioned by a knowledge of God's word. I therefore hoped by this effort to utilize my own Bible knowledge by sharing lessons from God's word to help us both increase our Bible knowledge, and therefore to provide strength and comfort we all need to face life.

I also had hoped to make these lessons contain a somewhat more in-depth approach to Scripture. This was in part to challenge myself, as well as to challenge the reader, in the hope of helping us grow by a perhaps deeper knowledge of God's word. These lessons were also intended to be short, to provide a lesson that can be read quickly, yet hopefully also give us spiritual substance to ponder throughout the day. The original design of these lessons was that they be a daily lesson, delivered on Monday through Friday. The Friday lesson was always on the subject of worship, as Christians look forward to gathering on the first day of the week. Since this work is now to include each day of the week, and is not based on a particular calendar, the reader may notice that about every five days the lesson is on a general or specific topic related to worship.

It is ironic that God's word is a closed book (Jude 3; Rev 22:18–19), and yet the pursuit of the knowledge of God's word should be a never-ending quest (2 Pet 3:18). It is hoped that this work may make some contribution toward a better understanding of God's word as well as to help the reader view life in a way that will bring them closer to God—that is, spiritually.

David Musgrave
Milford, Ohio

January 1
"Perfect Peace"

ISAIAH 26:3 READS "A sustained mindset you will protect with a perfect peace, because he is trusting in you." This tells us that God will keep in "perfect peace" the one who has his mind sustained by God. The phrase "perfect peace" is in Hebrew "peace, peace." It is therefore emphatic, as when a salesperson says "for the low, low price of . . ." To keep our mind set on God gives us a peace we cannot know otherwise—a perfect peace.

January 2

"Set Your Mind"

As CHRISTIANS WE NEED to constantly keep our mental focus on spiritual things. Paul said, "Set your minds on things that are above, not on things that are on earth" (Col 3:2). To do this requires both purpose (we have to decide to do it) and consistency (we need to do it regularly). The word translated "set" is a command (an imperative in Greek), so it is something we must determine to do. When we follow this teaching, earthly things will take on less importance, and we will be spiritually stronger.

January 3

"Trust in the Lord"

Proverbs 3:5–6 reads, "Trust in the Lord with all your heart and do not lean on your understanding. Know him in all your ways, and he for his part will make your paths straight." We need to trust God no matter what it means. The wise man gives us the spiritual element ("with all your heart"), and what it will mean for our lives ("he will make your paths straight"). By again concentrating on spiritual things, the physical things take on less importance whether things go our way or not.

January 4
The Enemy of Worry

WORRY SHOULD BE A bigger enemy than the thing about which we are worried. This is because while problems cause pain and can be detrimental to life and happiness, worry is detrimental to our soul. The word "anxiety" has to do with fear (the German word *Angst* means "fear"). Several Scriptures show that fear is the opposite of faith (Matt 14:30; 1 Kgs 17:13). We overcome fear by spiritual means, such as prayer, Bible study, and contemplating Scripture. Whether our physical problems persist, we will by doing these things gain something more valuable, a stronger spiritual life.

January 5
Reading Spiritually

ONE OF MY TEACHERS used to say, partly in fun, "Who reads Chronicles?" Books like Chronicles and other sections in the Bible that consist of such things as genealogies may seem to have a purpose the reader today has trouble understanding. Yet, since we believe the Bible is inspired, we can assume that such things are in the Bible for a reason. When we read the Bible with a spiritual mindset (that is, with regard to what it means, what I can learn for the good of my soul, etc.), it will make more spiritual sense and be more applicable to our (spiritual) lives.

January 6

"I Have Learned"

LEARNING IS USUALLY HARD work. Whether it be a lesson brought on by experience, or the hard work of having to study in school, learning takes work and is sometimes painful. Paul's words in Phil 4:12 serve as a reminder that growing as a Christian is often painful. "I know how to be brought low, and I know how to abound. In any and every circumstance, I have learned the secret of facing plenty and hunger, abundance and need." Yet, these words also tell us that difficult circumstances can be for our spiritual good, depending on our response. Often the only way to gain this good is by going through the learning experience of difficult circumstances (2 Cor 12:10).

January 7

The Mindset We Choose

In Luke 12:29 Jesus said, "And seek not ye what ye shall eat, and what ye shall drink, neither be ye of doubtful mind" (ASV). Attitude is something we choose. To not be "of doubtful mind" includes not worrying, as reflected in other translations (the Greek word has a literal meaning of being "in a tizzy"). This means that, to follow this teaching, we have to choose to trust God. The same thought is expressed by Paul in Phil 2:5, when he said to "have this mind in you." The mindset we have is the mindset we choose.

January 8

One of Two Ways

Psalm 1 is often interpreted as an introduction to the book of Psalms. It sets before the reader a choice of two ways in life. Verse 1 seems to present a progression to the association one might have with evil: "Blessed is the one who does not walk by the advice of (the) wicked, nor stand in the way of (the) sinners, nor sit in the seat of (the) scornful" (Ps 1:1). That is, one is blessed if they do not "walk . . . nor stand . . . nor sit." Each of these actions is not only a choice, but also shows that we often have several opportunities to stop our association with evil before evil becomes part of us.

January 9

"Never Leave or Forsake"

IN HEB 13:5 GOD repeated the promise to not "leave nor forsake" his children. He had said the same thing several times before, including to Joshua (Josh 1:5). Both words, *leave* and *forsake*, have basically the same meaning, that of "abandon." Why would God use the same word twice? Perhaps to reinforce that this, like the promise of "perfect peace" (see Isa 26:3) is something we can count on?

January 10
I Believe God

IN THE MIDDLE OF a storm at sea, Paul told the others on the ship that an angel of God had spoken to him, and that he believed God (Acts 27:25). Paul chose to believe what God said. He didn't wait to be persuaded, or for a feeling to come over him. For Paul it was a message direct from an angel of God; for us it is the written word (Heb 1:1–2). Especially when we find ourselves in the middle of a storm (or even just going along in a routine life) recalling God's message, and believing it, in other words looking at life spiritually rather than physically, will help us through the storm.

January 11

"We Ought Always to Pray"

PRAYER IS AN EXERCISE that does the prayer spiritual good, among other things. If we look at prayer primarily as a means of getting something or as a way to fix a problem, we may be looking at it incorrectly. Jesus said that we "ought always to pray, and not to faint" (Luke 18:1). This reminds us that it's important to pray for our spiritual good, and that the physical situation that we're praying about is perhaps secondary.

January 12

"My Help Comes from the Lord"

IN PS 121:1 THE psalmist asked, "I will lift my eyes to the mountains; from where will my help come?" By asking from where his help will come, the psalmist is in effect expressing a cry that he needs help. He goes on to state, "My help comes from the LORD, maker of heaven and earth." He then emphasizes that God is his helper by saying that God will "keep" his people, using a form of the (Hebrew) word "keep" six times in this short psalm. God keeps his children, even when we feel like we need to ask for help.

January 13

"But God Intended"

In Gen 50:20 Joseph told his brothers, "Now as for you, you intended evil against me, but God intended it for good." God can cause any situation to work together for some good purpose (Rom 8:28), even if people intend an evil purpose. Among other things, this tells us not only of the futility of worry, but it also gives us comfort in the controlling providence of God for good in the midst of evil circumstances.

January 14
Ready for Anything

Though we don't know and can't know the future, being mentally and spiritually prepared can help us deal with difficult circumstances; and difficult circumstances are going to come in life. Thus the Bible contains teaching regarding being ready to preach (Rom 1:15), being prepared to face temptation (Dan 1:8), and being generally prepared with a strong mind (1 Pet 1:13). One way to be prepared is to accept the fact that difficulties are going to come and then use that as a means of developing trust in God. The psalmist said, "Even though I should walk through the valley of the shadow of death . . ." (Ps 23:4). Having faith in God includes accepting whatever is going to happen.

January 15

"Casting on Him"

Do you ever complain to someone besides God, perhaps over and over, about the same thing? Do they get tired of hearing it? While we are to do all things without complaining (Phil 2:14), we need someone to take our troubles to. Not only does God encourage us to come to him (Heb 4:16), but we are indirectly discouraged from unloading on others. Peter thus taught "casting all your anxieties on him" (1 Pet 5:7). When looking for someone to whom we take our troubles, if we take them to the One whose ear never gets tired, think of how much we would spare those whose ears do get tired.

January 16
"We Know"

SEVERAL TIMES THE BIBLE speaks of our knowing certain truths with a phrase such as "we know." This reflects that there are some truths in the Christian life that are understood to be true. Some of these include that all things work together for good to those that love God (Rom 8:28); that Christians are in a right relationship with God (1 John 2:3), and therefore have eternal life (1 John 5:13). For Christians it is comforting to know not just that there are truths that can be acquired, but that we know and can know these truths.

January 17
Evangelism or Evangelistic?

DOES GOD DESIRE HIS children to do evangelism or to be evangelistic? The answer to this may not be either/or; yet it may be helpful to ask whether evangelism is a job we complete or a characteristic that defines us. Some jobs (like replacing a new roof) have to be completed as soon as possible. Knowing that every hour souls are lost for all eternity emphasizes the urgency of evangelism (Matt 28:18–20). Perhaps, as a way of helping us do it, we should concentrate on being evangelistic (i.e., develop this characteristic within ourselves), rather than "getting the job done." Maybe both?

January 18
Waiting for Energy

LIVING LIFE WITH A spiritual approach (doing such things as praying without ceasing, meditating on Scripture, etc.) can give one physical energy. Negative thoughts take away energy; positive thoughts give energy. Perhaps this is included in Isa 40:31, "but those who wait for the LORD will renew (their) strength; they will raise their pinions like the eagles; they will run and not grow weary; they will walk and not become faint." In other words, "godliness is of value in every way" (1 Tim 4:8).

January 19

Homeless but Hopeful

Having been blessed to have never been truly homeless, it's hard to imagine how it must feel to find oneself in that condition. I have heard that one of the hardest things about being homeless is the feeling of hopelessness, that one has no idea where they will sleep or from where their next meal will come. The Christian is assured that, whether they have a permanent physical home or not, they do have hope. God promises that he will provide for our needs (Phil 4:19), and that we can hope beyond this life (1 Pet 1:3), because we can look forward to going home to be with God in heaven (2 Cor 5:1).

January 20

"Lead to Repentance"

WHAT IS IT THAT causes one to repent before God? The answer to this may not be only one thing. Fear can be a motivator, such as in life, the fear of loss can motivate one with regard to their finances. In the Bible, fear can prompt one to repent ("but unless you repent, you will all likewise perish," Luke 13:3). But the Bible also speaks of positive things, such as "God's kindness is meant to lead you to repentance" (Rom 2:4). Such things as the possibility of forgiveness, blessings for which we thank God, and the resolution of a problem, can seemingly soften the heart and lead one to repentance. For repentance to occur would seem to depend both on the nature of the kindness and, perhaps especially, on the heart affected thereby.

January 21
Missing Worship

Do we miss worshiping God in the presence of other Christians? One may or may not miss getting dressed, driving to the building, sitting for an hour or two, etc. Is it possible to not miss what is required physically, but to miss what it means spiritually (worshiping God, edification, learning, etc.)? Perhaps this is a good parallel to life itself—that is, living the Christian life has challenges (2 Tim 2:12) but also brings joy (Gal 5:22) because of what it means (a strong spiritual life, being with our brethren to worship God, eternity at the end, etc.). In heaven we will worship God for all of eternity (see Rev 4:8). Knowing this could change our attitude toward what it means to worship God in the meantime on earth.

January 22

Sin Enslaves; Truth Sets Free

JESUS SAID THAT SIN enslaves, and that truth sets us free (John 8:31–36). Truth is something that can be attained ("you shall know the truth"), and yet is also something we should continually pursue (2 Pet 3:18). To strive for truth on a regular basis is therefore to work our way out of slavery. Unlike a prison run by men, the pursuit of truth, if we go about it properly, will ultimately set our soul free by helping us to be right with God. By studying and learning God's word (John 17:17) on a regular basis we can have spiritual freedom, a blessing we can attain in no other way.

January 23

Hurry Home

IN LUKE 15:18 THE prodigal son states, "I will arise and go to my father," after which Luke states "and he arose, and came (v. 20)." The two words "arise and go/come" are a way of stating that he hurried. The same expression appears in Gen 27:19, with the second word being "sit down" (otherwise the meaning would be "arise, sit down"). The phrase is used of Phillip in Acts 8:26–27, when an angel told Phillip to go south, and of Jonah in Jonah 1:2 when God gave him his charge. Perhaps this urgency was because the prodigal had had enough of his wayward lifestyle. Perhaps he was in enough pain that he knew his days were numbered if he stayed there. In any case, he seems to have known, after he "came to himself," that he could hurry home to his father. And he was right, because the father "saw him afar off" (v. 20) as if he was looking for him. Looking for him to hurry home.

January 24
Watch That First Step

THE OPENING VERSE OF Ps 1 again gives us insight both into how to walk through the psalms, as well as how to take careful steps in life. The progression of "does not walk . . . nor stand . . . nor sit" shows us that Hebrew poetry is written in parallel lines. It also shows us that since our first step leads to a second, we therefore have to be careful in life what that first step will be. If, like Peter, we warm ourselves by the wrong fire (Mark 14:54), the next thing we know we'll be denying the Lord (Mark 14:71). Better to avoid being near sinful things by determining to beforehand (Dan 1:8) by fleeing them (1 Tim 6:10), and thereby avoid a possible sinful outcome (Jas 1:14–15).

January 25
Building Endurance

THE NT WORD OFTEN translated "endurance" or "steadfastness" has a meaning of bearing up under something, more so than of simply waiting. Life is not easy, in that we all have burdens to bear. As a rule, if we are a little harder on ourselves, life will be a little easier for us. One of the best things Christians can do is to bear up under the difficulties of life, or be "steadfast." We gain the ability to do this by a strong spiritual life. Such things as spending time in prayer and Bible study, putting the Bible into practice in life (Heb 5:14), and developing a hope in something better (Rom 5:4) give us a strength in our soul that helps us endure, or bear up under, the burdens that might otherwise cause us to crumble.

January 26

"Without Ceasing"

To "PRAY WITHOUT CEASING" (1 Thess 5:17) includes the idea of keeping up one's prayer life. Prayer can certainly be an asset at many times in life, and therefore "without ceasing" can also mean at any or every turn in the road. In Neh 2:4 the king asked Nehemiah why he was so sad and what he wanted. Before he answered the king Nehemiah said, "So I prayed to the God of heaven." Whether we have to speak to someone in authority, or we are facing a tremendous challenge or problem, if we pray, we can be brought closer to God and possibly receive help in our time of need (Heb 4:16).

January 27
Good to Have Goals

It is good to have goals. Goals give us something to work toward, something to get excited about, and a reason to not get bogged down in the past or the present (though all of these can serve some purpose). Paul said, "But one thing I do: forgetting what lies behind and straining forward to what lies ahead, I press on toward the goal for the prize of the upward call of God in Christ Jesus" (Phil 3:13–14). The Greek word translated "goal" is from where we get the English word "scope," as in "scope out." For Christians the ultimate goal we scope is that of heaven, the goal we have our sights on, are striving for, and are looking forward to attaining. If it's good to have goals, that means it's good that we don't have everything we want on the way to achieving our goals. On we go.

January 28
Better Through Use

NOT MANY THINGS IN life improve by using them. Hammers, running shoes, and hard drives wear out over time. Even the human body, amazingly as it functions, wears out over time. In 1 Tim 4:8 Paul said, "Bodily training is of some value." The spirit, however, can improve (2 Cor 4:16). By using the word (Heb 5:14) we can become stronger in spirit, more knowledgeable in thought, and wiser in deduction. We do this by input, application, and consistency. We do this by concentrating on something that makes us better—God's word.

January 29
He Redeemed Us

THE IDEA OF REDEMPTION means we are not obligated to pay a price for which we otherwise would be responsible. When we redeem a coupon at the store, it doesn't mean nobody has to pay the one dollar off; it means we don't have to pay the one dollar off, but a price still has to be paid. With regard to sin, Jesus' being beaten to within an inch of his life, then hanging on a piece of wood until he had no more life, is the price that was paid (Eph 1:7). If he hadn't done this, Christians would be responsible for the price of their sins. But as it is, he redeemed us—he paid the price.

January 30
"Redeeming the Time"

THE VERB TRANSLATED "TO redeem" only appears four times in the NT. It appears twice with regard to Christ redeeming Christians (Gal 3:13 and 4:5). The other two times are with regard to Christians making the most of their time. These two passages are Eph 5:16 ("redeeming the time, because the days are evil" ASV) and Col 4:5 ("walk in wisdom toward them that are without, redeeming the time" (ASV). Like any price, this is an investment in something better. While Christ paid the necessary price for our eternal good (see yesterday's "Daily"), we are to pay the price to make the most of time and opportunity. To do so helps us get the most out of life but is also good for our spiritual life, as we can thereby bring glory to the eternal God.

January 31

"According to the Power"

PAUL DESCRIBED GOD AS one who is "able to do far more abundantly than all that we ask or think," yet is also working "according to the power at work within us" (Eph 3:20). This suggests that God's doing things beyond our comprehension is constrained by the extent to which the power is at work within us. Elsewhere Paul refers to the gospel as "the power" (Rom 1:16). Perhaps God will do "far more abundantly" than we could think if more of our thoughts were according to his word.

February 1
"See..."

DEVELOPING TRUST IN GOD includes the idea that we accept whatever is going to happen. Yet when our requests have to do with something we desperately want or need, we can use that desire to develop this trust by believing that God has given us what we ask for. The purpose of this is not just to get what we want, but to develop our faith. Several verses illustrate this principle: In Josh 6:2, God told Joshua, "See, I have given Jericho into your hand" before it fell. In Mark 11:24 Jesus said, "Therefore I tell you, whatever you ask in prayer, believe that you have received it, and it will be yours." Disappointment can be avoided by leaving the results up to God (Matt 26:39). Faith can be developed by seeing the results first.

February 2
The Desires of Your Heart

ONE OF THE KEYS to receiving our heart's desire is to change our heart. The psalmist said, "And take pleasure in the LORD, so that he would give you your heartfelt requests" (Ps 37:4). The Hebrew word translated "take pleasure in" has a basic meaning of "to be soft toward." This is not a magic formula; but, based on this verse, what God wants is for our heart to be a certain way, more so than to simply give us what we want. Satisfying our heart's desire begins with delighting in our heart toward God.

February 3

Overcome Evil

ACCOMPLISHING GOOD IN LIFE usually requires effort. If we don't tend our garden, the weeds will take over. If we do nothing with regard to our health, it could deteriorate more quickly. Evil also has a way of finding us whether we are looking for it or not (the Bible speaks of Satan walking about looking for us, 1 Pet 5:8). An answer to overcoming evil includes such things as fleeing evil (Jas 4:7), seeking peace (Ps 34:14), and being "rich in good works" (1 Tim 6:18). Evil can be overcome (Rom 12:21); but to do so includes our doing good, which usually doesn't happen on its own.

February 4
A Growing Building

BUILDINGS ARE INANIMATE THINGS that have to be built and rebuilt (they don't rebuild themselves). Kings in the ancient world were concerned with their being recognized as the one who built or rebuilt certain monuments, structures, and cities. The church is described as a building that grows (Eph 2:21). It was built (v. 20; Matt 16:18), and it is to continue to grow. Unlike buildings that require materials and labor not to grow, but simply to remain standing, the church grows by being supported with spiritual material (1 Cor 3:10–15). When she does, she becomes a "holy temple" built by the King, wherein he is pleased to dwell (Eph 2:22).

February 5
The Right Words

WE NEVER NEED TO worry about expressing ourselves properly to God. From a linguistic viewpoint, it can be true when someone says "I didn't mean to say that." This is because in speaking, the thoughts come first, after which we search for the right words; and sometimes we either don't have the right word, or we choose the wrong word (for evidence, listen to a young child who is trying to convey their thoughts, but hasn't yet learned enough words). God already knows what we need (Matt 6:32). In process of speaking to him, the Holy Spirit helps convey our thoughts to God (Rom 8:26). A purpose of prayer, then, could be not to inform God, but to engage in a spiritual exercise that brings us closer to God (Luke 18:1–8), even if we may use the wrong words.

February 6
Don't Quit

QUITTING IS ONE OF the few actions that ensures a certain outcome. If we begin an academic degree, a business venture, or a building project, there is no guarantee that we are going to be successful (Luke 14:28–30). But if we quit, we will not gain the benefit we had set out to achieve. There may be times when we have to change direction in life, or even quit a task (1 Tim 1:20). Spiritually, we are walking toward something in life. In the Christian life, it is important not just that we walk, but that we walk in a certain way. This includes walking worthily of the gospel (Eph 4:1; the Greek word translated "worthy" is from where our English word *axle* comes), that is, in a way corresponding to the gospel we were taught, and even to increase in our efforts. Thus Paul said, "As you received from us how you ought to walk and to please God, just as you are doing, that you do so more and more" (1 Thess 4:1). In other words, don't quit.

February 7

Protected by Peace

SEVERAL TIMES IN THE Bible military images are used with regard to God's watchful care over his children. In Phil 4:7 Paul said that the result of replacing worry with prayer will be "and the peace of God, which surpasses all understanding, will guard your hearts and your minds in Christ Jesus." The Greek word translated "guard" is one such military term, meaning to protect, as in a military garrison. While such spiritual and emotional enemies as worry can do us harm, the peace of God stands guard over us to keep us safe. Christians are protected by the peace of God.

February 8

Seeking the Lost

Much is involved when looking for something that is lost—the time that we never get back, the emotions (maybe being upset because of the importance of what you're looking for) and perhaps, depending upon whether one finds it, the joy when it is found. To return to the prodigal son, his father said that he "was lost and is found" (Luke 15:24), and called his household to celebrate (v. 23). The blessing of something positive like this usually has a greater impact after a time of deprivation (such as something good to eat or drink after doing without). To pursue pleasure is the wrong path in life (1 Tim 5:6). To strive for better in the hope of attaining, while sometimes doing without in this life, is an end toward which Christians are to strive (Luke 13:24). How pleasurable it will be when our efforts end with a resolution of pain (Rev 21:4) and the final restoration of that which had been lost. A time to celebrate indeed.

February 9
This World Is Not Our Home

THOUGH IT CAN SOMETIMES be a challenge, we are able to adapt to our surroundings. When Israel was displaced to Babylon for seventy years, many Israelites adapted, not wishing to return home to rebuild their temple and their way of life. If Christians become too comfortable in this world by loving it (1 John 2:15), by close association with it (1 Cor 15:33), or by being a friend of it (Jas 4:4), we may forget wherein our true allegiance lies. Paul said, "But our citizenship is in heaven, and from it we await a Savior, the Lord Jesus Christ" (Phil 3:20). While we can adjust to the oddities of life on this plane (Phil 4:12), we should remember that this is all going to end one day, at which time Christians will go home (1 Thess 4:17). If we remember this, the world and all of its features will take on less importance. And, like Jesus (John 17), we can look forward to going home.

February 10
"He Meditates"

THE MIND IS ALWAYS active. In the course of our day we think about many necessary things, including meals, work-related problems, etc. Are there moments wherein we can think about something else? In Ps 1:1–2, the blessed one is he who "meditates" on God's instruction "day and night": "but his delight is in the LORD's instruction; so he meditates on His instruction day and night." The Hebrew word translated "meditates" carries an idea of "uttering" (it doesn't necessarily have to consist of closing one's eyes in deep contemplation). One does this "day and night," or all the time. While it is necessary for our thoughts to be engaged with mundane things, we could use moments throughout the day to meditate on God's instruction. To do so would offer a distraction from this world and, more importantly, give us spiritual strength by drawing closer to God.

February 11

"Be Strong"

THERE IS A DIFFERENCE between "being" and "becoming" (or "affect" and "effect"). Paul said, "Be strong in the Lord" (Eph 6:10). To become suggests changing, such as becoming thinner or more humble. To be suggests we use a quality we already have, such as "be careful" or "be diligent." Instead of becoming stronger (which is also possible, 2 Cor 4:16), Paul says Christians are to utilize a strength they already have, as they draw from their spiritual reserve built up through prayer and Bible study. A physical reserve will eventually fail us; to be strong in the strength that God supplies will equip us for spiritual battle.

February 12
Stop Fretting over Evil

WE OFTEN WONDER WHY there is such a thing as evil, and why evil seems to persist. Since there is evil, Christians must be careful how we think about it. One quality we should avoid with regard to evil is that of anger. In Ps 37:1–10, the psalmist said three times not to "fret" (or be angry) over evildoers (vv. 1, 7, 8; the Hebrew phrase translated "do not fret" has the idea of "stop fretting"). The reason the psalmist gives is that evil will eventually be addressed (ended) by God, while spiritual qualities such as righteousness and justice will endure (v. 6). Since anger can cause us to sin (Eph 4:26), and it is as difficult to be angry and not sin as it is rare (Ps 37:8), the best thing to do is to put it away (Eph 4:31), or stop fretting over, evil.

February 13
A Blessing in Disguise

CAN SOMETHING UNPLEASANT BE a blessing? There are unpleasantries in life (maybe more than the pleasantries). One advantage the Christian has in this regard is the perspective we bring to something negative. Difficult experiences can be positive because of their spiritual effect. After requesting and being denied the removal of a "thorn in the flesh," Paul said, "therefore I will boast all the more gladly of my weaknesses, so that the power of Christ may rest upon me" (2 Cor 12:9). When something negative in life befalls, it may be that a "blessing in disguise" is therefore a blessing in plain sight.

February 14
True Liberation with Truth

TRUTH IS TODAY A scarce commodity, as it has always been. Truth is one of the few things that will solve many political, emotional, and especially spiritual problems; yet it is one of the main things not many seem to want. An old saying is that the further one goes from the truth, the angrier they become when their belief is challenged. True liberation comes from accepting the truth. Jesus said, "And you will know the truth, and the truth will set you free" (John 8:32). While other things such as legitimate pleasures may provide temporary escape, only truth sets us free. If we begin from the right place, that God's word is truth (John 17:17), and never cease pursuing truth, we will end up in the right place—liberated!

February 15

Not Like It Is Here

MANY TIMES, SUCH AS when trying to describe the sunrise, words are inadequate. Sometimes the Bible describes heaven in terms of what it is not like on earth. Peter referred to the Christian's inheritance in heaven as "imperishable, undefiled, and unfading, kept in heaven for you" (1 Pet 1:4). On good days we may like the idea of life going on forever. On bad days we may realize that the negative aspects of life can make us long for something better. God tells his children there is something better—a place that's not like it is here.

February 16
The New Normal

THE IDEA OF A "new normal" suggests one's having to adjust to a new way of life. Sin is not normal, as it is not the way God intended for humans to live (Gen 2:16–17). Paul told the Corinthians that "neither the sexually immoral, nor idolaters, nor adulterers, nor men who practice homosexuality, nor thieves, nor the greedy, nor drunkards, nor revilers, nor swindlers will inherit the kingdom of God" (1 Cor 6:9–10). He then said "And such were some of you. But you were washed, you were sanctified, you were justified in the name of the Lord Jesus Christ and by the Spirit of our God" (1 Cor 6:11). In other words, since Christians have been made new (2 Cor 5:17), they are to live according to a new standard. Living without sin is the way God intended humans to live in the beginning. So for one who is now a Christian, new is normal.

February 17

Always True

THE NT WORD FOR "truth" has to do with things that do not change (the Greek word so translated means "without forgetfulness"). It tells us that some ideas are always true and do not depend on what one thinks about them. Many delight in something simply because it is new or because it makes them feel good. The Greek philosophers Paul spoke to in Acts 17 spent their time in nothing else but "to tell or to hear some new thing" (v. 21; even though their hero Plato would have called people like this "a strange lot"). What they did not want was truth. To be able to receive truth begins in attitude, one which causes our ears to be directed toward it rather than away from it (2 Tim 4:4). If we do this we will find it (Matt 7:7), since it doesn't change.

February 18
"God's Word Is Able"

God's word is one of the most powerful tools we have at our disposal. While many other things (such as prayer) are also powerful, God's word is powerful to change people's hearts. As Paul was planning to leave the elders of Ephesus he commended them "to God and to the word of his grace, which is able to build you up and to give you the inheritance among all those who are sanctified" (Acts 20:32). While words can incite violence, words can also accomplish positive good. God's word can build up. As Christians we therefore have one of the most powerful tools, to help fix the most complex problems, those of the heart. What will our parting word be?

February 19
Humbling to Be Exalted

When one has the right attitude, it is humbling to be exalted. As Christians, we are going to be humble. Either we humble ourselves, in which case God will exalt us; or we exalt ourselves, and God will humble us (Luke 14:11). Either way we are going to be humble. It's a lot more fun to be exalted than to try to exalt ourselves, and it's much more painful to be humbled. Peter said, "Humble yourselves, therefore, under the mighty hand of God so that at the proper time he may exalt you" (1 Pet 5:6). The keys in this verse include truly humbling ourselves from the heart and having patience to wait for God to exalt us in the proper time—his time. In other words, to get what we want, in this case greatness, we are to relinquish our desire for it, or humble ourselves.

February 20

"Like a Father"

When Paul described his work with the Thessalonians in terms of fatherhood, he gave insight both into how a father is to fill his role, as well as what the ultimate goal of fatherhood should be. Paul said, "For you know how, like a father with his children we exhorted each one of you and encouraged you and charged you to walk in a manner worthy of God, who calls you into his own kingdom and glory" (1 Thess 2:11). Of the things Paul mentions here, the last has to do with being right with God. While proper fathers often want what is physically best for their child, the ultimate goal should be what is spiritually best. To accomplish this a father should concentrate on spiritual things as they raise their child. While therefore it's not necessarily wrong for a father to want his child to be a professional baseball player or a CEO of a corporation, what he should also want, and should work toward, is that his children be Christians, or walk in a manner worthy of God. The ultimate goal for the role of father is spiritual.

February 21

"Wings Like Eagles"

WOULDN'T IT BE WONDERFUL to soar like an eagle above our problems? Though we can't physically fly like a bird, we can fly above through a feeling of excitement that comes from concentrating on spiritual things. Isaiah 40:31 again states, "But those who wait for the LORD will renew (their) strength; they will raise their pinions like the eagles; they will run and not grow weary; they will walk and not become faint." The Hebrew word translated "wait" has a connotation of eagerness, such as the feeling of anticipation when waiting on something we desperately want. This tells us that we can take delight in not having what we want or that we can use this feeling for spiritual good. In other words, not having what we want can help us wait for the Lord; that is, we can soar like an eagle.

February 22

"Corrupting Talk"

WHAT IS "CORRUPTING TALK"? Paul said, "Let no corrupting talk come out of your mouths, but only such as is good for building up, as fits the occasion, that it may give grace to those who hear" (Eph 4:29). What defines "cursing" (cussing) has changed over the last century and is also different between cultures. The word Paul used for "corrupting" has a meaning of putrefying. So while it may be hard to define, bad language can be recognizable to the spiritually minded (similar to the child who asked his mother what a rotten egg smells like, and she said, "If you ever come across one, you'll know it"). The Christian has no list of approved or unapproved speech in the Bible, but rather is to decide based on spiritual reasons (such things as whether their speech builds up and is gracious, or properly seasoned, Col 4:6). If something is putrefied it can't be seasoned enough to make it palatable. So it is best not to use such speech at all.

February 23
Anywhere I Go

ONE WAY TO SPEAK of absolutely everything (and everything in between) is to use a figure of speech meaning "from one end to another." So in the OT we have the phrase "Dan to Beersheba" (1 Sam 3:20), meaning from one end of Palestine to the other, and Gen 1:1, "the heavens and the earth," meaning everything. The psalmist said, "If I were to ascend to heaven, there You are. And should I lay in Sheol, here you are" (Ps 139:8). This tells us that there is nowhere we can go where God is not. To one who does not desire to do right before God this can be an unpleasant reality (John 3:20); but for those who walk in the light it is comforting to know that we can hide from men, we can hide from ourselves, but we can't hide from God. It is not good for us to be alone (Gen 2:18); as Christians we are not.

February 24
Too Bad

THE WORD *WOE* IS another figure of speech (onomatopoeia) that is used to represent a sound (in this case a wailing). When used in the Bible it means that it will be too bad for the one spoken of. For the world to call Christians "evil" and others, such as those who do violence, as "good" is the opposite of truth. Such seems to be an attempt to legitimize a lifestyle or to have a wrong belief accepted. Isaiah stated it: "Alas (to) those who proclaim evil good and good evil, who put darkness for light and light for darkness, bitter for sweet and sweet for bitter!" (Isa 5:20). While it can be aggravating and even frightening to know that one who is trying to do the right thing would be called "evil," it seems important to remember that this verse is a warning to those who label everything as its opposite. So while they may be able to fool others by renaming good and evil, they are not fooling God; too bad for them.

February 25

Enjoyable Worship

WORSHIP CAN BE ENJOYABLE without being fun. Fun (as here defined) is why we go to such things as amusement parks, concerts, and movies. Joy is a spiritual quality that we get from a spiritual life. Paul said that the fruit of the Spirit includes "love, joy, peace, patience, kindness, goodness, faithfulness, gentleness, self-control" (Gal 5:22–23). Worship is a spiritual activity that is directed to God to bring glory to him (John 4:24) among other things. When we engage in worship from the heart it brings us closer to him, and therefore can bring us joy. While there can be fun in worship (such as a well-turned bit of humor), by directing our spiritual efforts to God we in turn build up our spiritual life or our fruit of the Spirit, which brings us joy; it makes such activity enjoyable.

February 26

"With All Your Heart"

IT MIGHT BE EASY to trust someone a little. We often like to be able to control and to fix things ourselves; yet getting life to "work" is not the primary objective of the Christian life. When the wise man said, "Trust in the LORD with all your heart and do not lean upon your understanding" (Prov 3:5), he is telling the child of God the attitude he is to bring to life's situations. He is not telling the reader what to do in life, but the attitude with which to approach life. The physical effort we put forth to get life to work can and should be to the utmost (Jas 2:24; Col 3:23). But while we do so the spiritual approach we bring to our efforts should be that we are trusting in God for all things, including the outcome of our efforts. In other words, it is to be with all of our heart.

February 27
God's Word Is Real

How real is God's word? Is it something lofty we listen to in order to make us feel good, or is it something powerful that can change life? For one's house or health to be damaged would be a reality he couldn't deny. In today's world, on the one hand one can be charged with a crime for using the wrong words; on the other hand children are exposed to foul language without their guardians even stopping to consider how it might affect them. In the Bible and the surrounding world words were considered real things. In Luke 20:20 some spies were sent to Jesus "that they might take hold of his speech" (ASV). First Samuel 3:19 states that the Lord was with Samuel, and that he "let none of his words fall to the ground." The gospel is the power of God (Rom 1:16) that can have a powerful effect on the heart (Heb 4:12). Let us treat it accordingly, as it won't return to God void (Isa 55:11). Let us not deny its power.

February 28
Getting Life to Work

To go through life, or get life to "work," we must put thought into it. Yet not every situation or problem has an easy solution; sometimes there is no solution. In addition to trusting in the Lord with all of our heart, the wise man also adds that one is not to rely on himself: "Trust in the Lord with all your heart and do not lean on your understanding" (Prov 3:5). To rely on ourselves alone suggests we are trying to succeed without God. The real solution is to leave the results up to God from our heart, or not rely on our understanding of how things will go. Life may or may not "work"; yet by trusting him we might grow closer to God in our heart, knowing that we are not alone.

February 29
A Straight Path

IN PROV 3:5–6, THE wise man again gave his readers a third thing to do when he said, "Know him in all your ways, and he for his part will make your paths straight" (v. 6). This reminds us of the need to look at life spiritually. While we again can and are to use our mind, and are to do all we can to be physically successful, our heart is to remain centered on God. When we do it will make the outcome of life's situations less important, whether we are successful or not. Both the words *ways* and *paths* can in the OT have a spiritual as well as a physical meaning. Since the word *straight* bears a meaning of "right," this shows that God will make one's life right before him. If the child of God keeps him in mind by acknowledging him, their path will be right because God has made our (his) path straight; even if it seems otherwise.

March 1

Going on Vacation

THE FEELING OF ANTICIPATION we often have before going on vacation is a combination of thinking about where we are going, with (which leads to) a feeling of excitement. As Christians we are to contemplate positive thoughts (Phil 4:8) in order, among other things, to store up a mental reserve. Setting our mind on heaven is like getting excited before going on vacation. Thus Paul taught us to so direct our mind in Col 3:2: "Set your minds on things that are above, not on things that are on earth." Thinking about leaving all of this behind, going to a place where there is no more pain (Rev 21:4), can motivate us by a feeling of excitement and anticipation. Except after this trip we don't have to return to work.

March 2

A Spiritual Reserve

AN UNEXPECTED FINANCIAL BURDEN is easier to handle mentally as well as financially when one has a reserve (even if they have to part with the money). Like building a financial reserve, we can also build a spiritual reserve to help us when unexpected burdens arise. The reserve we build is stored in our soul and therefore comes through our mind. Such verses as Phil 4:8 tell us to build this reserve: "Finally, brothers, whatever is true, whatever is honorable, whatever is just, whatever is pure, whatever is lovely, whatever is commendable, if there is any excellence, if there is anything worthy of praise, think about these things." The Greek word translated "think" literally means "to take account of," as if adding these thoughts to the bank account of our mind. Positive thoughts can help us feel better at the time we dwell on them and, through sustained contemplation, can also build a reserve. While we may not use this reserve today, it will give us something in our bank account to be able to pay the bill when taxing times come. And they will come.

March 3

When "Bad" Things Happen

WE CAN'T ALWAYS BASE our spiritual life on how our physical life goes. When hardships happen some conclude that they must have done something wrong, while others conclude that God must have done something wrong. When "bad" things make us unhappy, it doesn't necessarily mean that God is unhappy with us. The disciples asked Jesus about a man born blind in John 9:2, "Who sinned, this man or his parents, that he was born blind?" Jesus answered that it was neither, "but that the works of God might be displayed in him" (v. 3). We can use difficult times for our own spiritual strength, and to bring glory to God. In other words, we can make God happy instead of worrying about whether we're happy.

March 4

Planted So We Bloom

WHEN THE PSALMIST SAID that the blessed person is one who meditates on God's law day and night, he then said that the result of this is that he would be "like a tree planted by channels of waters, who will produce his fruit in his time, and whose leafage will not wither; and he will prosper in everything which he may do" (Ps 1:3). Being planted like a tree is something that is done for the child of God. While it's fine to pursue qualities we think we need (such as concentrating on being patient), if we concentrate on such things as meditating on God's word, God will plant us so that we bloom and bear spiritual fruit. This "fruit of the Spirit" (Gal 5:22–23) is not so much a reward, but rather a result of living a spiritual life based on God's word. Concentrate on the seed of God's word (Luke 8:11) and God will see to it that we are planted so we can grow.

March 5

"Ezra Had Set His Heart"

Ezra is said to be one who "had set his heart to study the instruction of the Lord, and to do it and to teach statutes and ordinances in Israel" (Ezra 7:10). There are three things Ezra is said to have done in this verse, the first of which is how he directed his heart. God's word is not lost; but in life things need to be sought, because they won't find us. More to the point, however, is the fact that Ezra's heart was set to learning the instruction of the Lord (this Hebrew word translated "study" means to seek, as one would study, that is for application). Ezra was a priest (Ezra 7:12), so we can assume he already knew God's word. Yet he set his heart to know it even better. Christians today are priests (1 Pet 2:5), and the Christian life is a life of learning, and therefore of seeking, God's word. If we treat God's word as a treasure to be sought (Matt 13:44), we will find it, and it will be worth the effort if we set our heart on it.

March 6

"If You Do Them"

PROPER KNOWLEDGE IS USUALLY essential to successful action, but action with improper knowledge could be harmful. While one is not saved by works (Eph 2:8–9), our knowledge as Christians is eventually to lead to a life of action, in such things as benevolence and evangelism. The second of three things Ezra is said to have done in Ezra 7:10, after saying that he "had set his heart to study the *torah* of the LORD," is that Ezra was said "to do it." Learning is an ongoing quest in the Christian life because no one has all of the answers. Yet learning and study is not the end of our quest. Just as a doctor studies so that he or she can help others with their health, so the Christian studies so that we can, among other things, put it into practice in life, for the ultimate purpose of bringing glory to God (Eph 1:12). In the words of Jesus, "If you know these things, blessed are you if you do them" (John 13:17).

March 7

Study and Teaching

BOTH STUDY AND ACTION should for the Christian be spiritual pursuits. Knowledge alone may be of little or no value if it is not based on truth (2 Tim 3:7); action alone can be of little value, especially if not carried out for the right reason (1 Tim 4:8). Both of these therefore should be spiritual and unselfish endeavors. The third thing Ezra the priest is said to have done, after stating that he had set his heart to study and to do the law of the Lord, is that he had also set his heart "to teach statutes and ordinances in Israel" (Ezra 7:10). A purpose of study is to influence our actions; a purpose of actions is to influence others so that we can, among other things, teach them. The purpose of all of this is to bring glory to God; these things are for spiritual purposes.

March 8

Being Content

FINDING A WAY TO be content can be difficult. We have desires and ambitions, and, as humans, tend to worry. Yet these emotions have to do with such temporal things as satisfying an appetite, receiving recognition, or realizing accomplishment. While these things can be good, such as when they give us proper motivation, to make these the only things we live for can result in negative fulfillment. God has given us the means to overcome all emotions that keep us from being satisfied. Hebrews 13:5 reads, "Keep your life free from love of money, and be content with what you have, for he has said, 'I will never leave you nor forsake you.'" Knowing that God is always there for us and will never, ever leave us provides a spiritual satisfaction that such things as money cannot. Rather than spending all of our efforts on things that cannot satisfy our soul, if we concentrate on spiritual things, we can be content. It isn't that difficult with God.

March 9

The Purpose of Prayer

Is the purpose of prayer only to ask God for things? While this is not wrong, and is even encouraged (John 16:24), a key to asking properly is that we do so with the right attitude. The psalmist said, "May the words of my mouth and the meditation of my heart be acceptable before you, O Lord, my rock and my redeemer" (Ps 19:14). This reminds us that prayer is not so much for the purpose of our getting what we want but is, like all acts of worship, primarily to please God. The more we strive to please God by our worship the more satisfied we will be and maybe get what we want. There is no single purpose of prayer.

March 10

"Preparing for Rain"

NOT ONLY DOES PREPARING for temptation help us to better resist it, but we as Christians can also prepare for God's showers of blessings. One story speaks of the farmer who trusted that God would provide, to the point that the farmer "prepared for rain." We can in like manner prepare for rain by expecting God to provide (Ezek 34:26). This is not to say that we can expect God to give us everything we want or even ask for; the fulfillment of our requests is still up to God's will (1 John 5:14). But a key ingredient in faith is believing that God will give us what we ask for whether we receive it or not (Mark 11:24). This includes believing that no matter the outcome of our prayers, it is good if it is in accordance with God's will. "Even though I should walk through the valley of the shadow of death . . ." (Ps 23:4). Prepare for a shower of blessing; our soul will be refreshed, whether the ground is or not.

March 11

Giving Up Our Will

ONE OF THE MAIN things God wants from us is our will. Jesus reflected this in his teaching (Matt 6:10) and in his last hours (Matt 26:42). While it's not wrong to get what we want, there can be many disadvantages, such as an unhealthy desire for more. Giving up our will is one thing God wants (John 6:38). Surely one reason he wants this is because this is what is best for us. One of the defining characteristics of love is that it is unselfish (1 Cor 13:5). Perhaps God wants us to relinquish our will because that's what he does for us—he loves us.

March 12

Conformed or Transformed

BEING CONFORMED TO SOMETHING may or may not be a good thing. Paul said, "Do not be conformed to this world" (Rom 12:2a). It is possible for one to pursue a sinful lifestyle, as well as to let a sinful lifestyle overtake them. The world often tries to make Christians live according to its sinful ways. Not so much because we're different, but because the world often doesn't like truth. Paul therefore says that the key to avoid letting ourselves be conformed to the world lies within in our mind: "but be transformed by the renewal of your mind, that by testing you may discern what is the will of God, what is good and acceptable and perfect" (Rom 12:2b). What do you think?

March 13

The Road of Truth

SOME TURN FROM THE truth because they have "itching ears" (2 Tim 4:3–4). Having an itch can be painful, but it is not necessarily wrong. Satisfying an itch could be wrong, depending on how we do it. Pursuing truth is a choice. But like scratching an itch, it can be both painful and pleasurable (when John was told to eat the scroll of God's revelation, the angel told him "Take and eat it; it will make your stomach bitter, but in your mouth it will be sweet as honey," Rev 10:9). Our decision to follow a teaching, whether spiritual, physical, or political, should be based in part on where it might lead us. Jesus said God's word is truth (John 17:17). Before we turn somewhere to be satisfied, let us ask whether the road we turn down will take us closer to God, whether it is the road of truth.

March 14

"Blessed to Give"

THE WORD BLESSING PROBABLY makes us think of something positive that we receive, especially if things go our way. In the Bible the word *bless* can also mean something the child of God offers back to him in the form of praise (Ps 103:1). In the Sermon on the Mount (Matt 5–7) Jesus said that the one who is blessed is one who has such characteristics as being "poor in spirit," "meek," "persecuted for righteousness' sake," etc. In other words, Jesus' criteria primarily have to do with our spirit adopting spiritual qualities from God. Rather than only receiving what we want, being blessed has more to do with our becoming like, and offering back to, God. We are blessed, not because we receive, but because we give. "It is more blessed to give than to receive" (Acts 20:35).

March 15

"Your Labor"

When Paul said, "in the Lord your labor is not in vain" (1 Cor 15:58), it reminds us again that the physical outcome of our efforts is not the most important thing. The saying "crime doesn't pay" is true (in part) because even if a criminal has a big score, they have done so at the expense of their, and possibly others,' soul. Whether we work "directly" for the Lord, or give our whole heart to our secular job because of Scripture teaching (Col 3:17), Paul's words can give the Christian motivation, including a reason to be persistent in our work. As Christians we will receive a reward for our labors (1 Cor 3:14), not necessarily because of our actions or their outcome, but because of the spiritual factors that guide our actions.

March 16

Reaching Out to God

MANY OF THE BLESSINGS God offers to his children depend on our reaching out to him first. Some examples include Jer 33:3, "Call to me, so that I may answer you, and report to you great and fortified things, which you do not know"; and Ps 37:4, "And take pleasure in the LORD, so that he would give you your heartfelt requests." God encourages us to come to him with our requests (Heb 4:16). But rather than asking for selfish reasons, it is again good to look at this practice spiritually. When we remember that satisfying our will is best left up to God's will, then these examples show us not that this is a magic formula for getting what we want, but is rather another key to developing our relationship with God. Getting what we want can be a means of giving God what he wants, that which is best for us.

March 17

Needs and Desires

DESIRES AND NEEDS ARE of course different and are often confused. One difference between them is that desires, even when satisfied, seem to arise again, often presenting a greater challenge to be satisfied. When Paul said, "And my God will supply every need of yours according to His riches in glory in Christ Jesus" (Phil 4:19), he was saying that God will see to our needs, not necessarily our desires; and that these will be completely taken care of. The Greek word translated "supply" literally means "to fill." Another need may afterward arise, and selfish desires can at best be only temporarily satisfied. We can rest assured that in Christ, that is, left in the realm of God's spiritual auspices, our needs are filled by God.

March 18

"He Will Laugh"

ONE OF THE FEW references in the Bible to God laughing is Ps 2:4, which reads, "The one who sits in the heavens will laugh; the LORD will mock them" (Ps 2:4). This verse portrays God as laughing at the nations who are rebelling against God and his anointed king (vv. 2–3). The nations surely think they can win, not realizing that God is in control. People's schemes, which are often based on arrogance, will ultimately fail because God is in control (Rom 13:1). To think otherwise is to give God a good laugh.

March 19

"A Light to Our Path"

WE NEED SOME WAY to illuminate our path in what can be a dark world. Our own understanding helps (Prov 3:5–6), but even we often don't know the best course. When God's light is shined on our path, it can illuminate for spiritual good. The psalmist said, "Your word is a lamp for my feet and a light for my path" (Ps 119:105). There will probably always be events and periods during which we can't see very clearly; but only God's word brings the necessary spiritual perspective of truth, so that we can see clearly to keep walking (Eph 4:1; 1 John 1:7). While walking this life we see through a mirror darkly (1 Cor 13:12); God's word is the light we need.

March 20

Through Jesus

Jesus said, "I am the way, and the truth, and the life. No one comes to the Father except through me" (John 14:6). While the lessons contained in this verse are many, one of the main ones is the logical conclusion that there is no way to be right with God except through Jesus (the Greek word translated "through" has the idea of "by the agency of"). Believing and following the truth of God's word provides us a path that leads to life. Other qualities such as honesty, sincerity, etc., may help one become a decent person. Only the "threefold cord" (Eccl 4:12) here spoken by Jesus is strong enough to make one right with God by giving one the means to climb to safety, to climb to heaven to be with God.

March 21

"At Peace with All"

THERE SEEM TO BE few directives in the Bible where God says for us to just do the best we can. When Paul said, "If possible, so far as it depends on you, live peaceably with all" (Rom 12:18), it reminds us that, as Christians, we are to do all we can, but that living peaceably with all may not be possible. Evil is looking for us (1 Pet 5:8), and must be withstood (Eph 6:11). Yet the Christian is to do their best to promote peace (Matt 5:9), especially the peace that comes from being right with God (Rom 5:1). We may not be able to be at peace with everybody; but God offers a peace that goes beyond our ability to understand (Phil 4:7). If more people had this peace we might be better able to live peaceably.

March 22

"So Walk in Him"

"Walking" in the Lord has to do with the way one lives their life, that is, spiritually. While there seem to be not many variations to walking for exercise, a spiritual life can take as many forms as there are varieties of teaching. Paul said that spiritual walking should consist of adhering to that which made one a Christian: "Therefore, as you received Christ Jesus the Lord, so walk in him" (Col 2:6). Receiving the Lord may be accompanied by emotions such as joy (Acts 8:39), thanksgiving (Col 2:7), etc., perhaps depending on the person; and all sinners who are converted to the Lord are done so with teaching (Rom 6:17). Continuing to walk in the Lord has to do with following this faith one was taught. While the Christian life includes growing in knowledge (2 Pet 3:18), one must stay with the teaching that brought them to a right relationship with God—the gospel.

March 23

Praying for Others

PRAYING FOR OTHERS DOES good. There are many reasons to pray. The Christian is to pray without ceasing (1 Thess 5:17) to pray for the governmental powers (1 Tim 2:1–4), and to pray simply to praise God (Matt 6:9). God encourages us to petition him with our own personal requests (Heb 4:16), but to ask for entirely selfish reasons is misguided (Jas 4:3). When the Bible tells us to pray for others, this reminds us that one of the benefits of this kind of prayer is that we will thereby not be thinking as much about ourselves. Whether those for whom we pray receive a direct benefit from our petitions or not, good is being done, that of our unselfishly concentrating on others.

March 24

"Where Was Your Faith?"

JESUS WAS SURPRISED AT his disciples that they were afraid during a storm (Matt 8:23–27). In life when we are hit with the occasional storm we have a choice, either fear or faith. Fear is again the opposite of faith and may be the natural way to react. Yet one cannot choose both. It may be difficult, and requires effort to not think about the negative circumstances. With practice (i.e., more storms, 2 Cor 12:10) we can develop a spiritual strength that helps us to look to Jesus in time of storm. The choice is ours; yet after the storm Jesus may ask, "Where was your faith?" (Luke 8:25).

March 25
Good to Be Afflicted

THE PSALMIST SAID, "IT is good for me to have been afflicted, in order that I may learn your statutes" (Ps 119:71). The Hebrew word translated "afflicted" has to do with being bowed down or humbled, such as can happen from many types of adversity. While the psalms are poetry, and therefore express ideals rather than more practical points, two ultimate truths can herefrom be gleaned: this verse suggests that the only way to observe good in a situation is by looking at the adversity spiritually; this verse also suggests that, at least for the psalmist, he would not have learned God's statutes otherwise. Thus the spiritual good of learning God's word is worth enduring affliction. Afflictions are going to come; what good will come about because of them?

March 26

A Reason to Hope

HOPE COMES FROM WITHIN. Even when one is given a glimmer of light in the midst of dark times, it is the spiritual qualities of the heart, that is, desire and expectation, that make the light meaningful. Again Paul said, "And endurance produces character, and character produces hope" (Rom 5:4). Hope is then another reason to welcome suffering, as this can have an effect on the heart. Regardless of how suffering affects one's physical life (Jesus said, "And do not fear those who kill the body but cannot kill the soul," Matt 10:28), the extent to which it can shape one's spiritual life gives the Christian a reason to rejoice and to endure. When a time of suffering comes, let us reshape our attitude toward it, by looking at the effect it has on our heart—the place from which hope arises.

March 27

The Power of Christ

WHEN PAUL SPOKE OF boasting in his weaknesses (referring to his own "thorn in the flesh"), he said that this was for a purpose: "But he said to me, 'My grace is sufficient for you, for my power is made perfect in weakness.' Therefore I will boast all the more gladly of my weaknesses, so that the power of Christ may rest upon me" (2 Cor 12:9). The purpose of Paul's boasting in his weaknesses was so that the power of Christ may rest upon him. This tells us that physical distresses can serve a spiritual purpose, which is that the power of Christ may rest upon us. While Paul doesn't tell us what the "power" is in this verse, he does say elsewhere that the gospel is the power of God (Rom 1:16). If we assume that this is (at least in part) what he means here, it tells us that one way to gain spiritual strength during a time of physical distress is by concentrating on God's word. By thinking about God's word instead of the money, the pain, or the problem of the moment, it can give us strength to endure, and possibly cause the "power of Christ" to rest upon us.

March 28

Learning and Knowledge

LEARNING AND KNOWLEDGE CAN both be either a good or a bad thing. Many people have knowledge of things that are not true. The Christian life is one of learning (the words *disciple* and *discipline* have to do with learning). Yet knowledge alone is not the goal. When in Hos 4:6 God said, "My people are ruined due to (their being) without knowledge," he was referring to their lack of knowledge of his word. The Christian life begins with believing the truth, and continues in a never-ending search thereof. The Christian is then the opposite of those of whom Paul spoke in 2 Tim 3:7, "always learning and never able to arrive at a knowledge of the truth." In the Christian life learning and knowledge are good things because it is based on truth.

March 29

Remember God's Word

IN THE BIBLE THE word *remember* often has the idea of "give attention to." In Gen 8:1, God hadn't forgotten about Noah and his family; when he "remembered" them, it means he gave attention to them. When we observe the Lord's Supper "in remembrance" of Jesus' death, it's not because we had forgotten that he died for us; the action of observing is in part to cause us to dwell on what Jesus did and all that it means for us. Luke 24:8 contains the simple statement "and they remembered his words." Recalling God's word can help us in many ways, including proper actions to follow (in these verses their remembering is followed by their returning from the tomb and telling these things to the rest of the apostles). Proper action is preceded by good thoughts. What better thoughts can we have than remembering God's word by giving attention thereto?

March 30

"In the Morning"

THE PSALMIST SPOKE OF bringing his petitions before God in the morning: "O LORD, in the morning you will hear my voice; in the morning I will lay (it) out for you and I will keep watch" (Ps 5:3). The psalmist doesn't say why he petitions God in the morning; yet, in the morning we expect to have the rest of the day before us. Thus he can say that he would set things in order before God, as if laying out his plans for the day. Rather than focus on his work and/or problems, his focus is on God. He thus states that he would watch closely (like a watchman, Isa 21:6). As the psalmist began his day he concentrated on things spiritual rather than physical, perhaps knowing that by concentrating on the spiritual the physical will be nothing to worry about (Matt 6:33–34). Certainly we can and should pray at any time (1 Thess 5:17). Yet what better time to lay out our petitions before God than when the day is new—in the morning?

March 31

"I Will Sing to the Lord"

The psalmist said, "let me sing to the Lord, because he has dealt generously with me" (Ps 13:6). When the psalmist states "let me," this has a sense of "don't you think I should?" His reason for singing to God is because he has "dealt generously" with him. Certainly sad times may cause us to want to sing a sad song; but an exuberance of heart, such as brought on by a fullness of life, can cause one to sing. The Hebrew word translated "dealt generously" appears in other verses with regard to produce ripening (Isa 18:5). Like a fruit tree in fall groaning under the weight of its produce, it is as if the psalmist has a similarly full heart, and this causes him to break forth in song to God. Rather than focusing only on himself and his desire for more, or his self-satisfaction, he recognizes the Source of his bounty, and he acts accordingly by giving glory to the One from whom bounty flows; that is to say, he sings.

April 1
"Added to You"

WHEN JESUS TAUGHT "BUT seek first the kingdom of God and His righteousness, and all these things will be added to you" (Matt 6:33), the Greek word translated "added" means "to set one thing around another" (it is the same word as in Acts 2:41, the Lord "added" to the number of the church). If we focus on things spiritual, the physical things such as what to eat and what to wear take on less importance (v. 31). Concentrating on the kingdom of God helps us in many ways, including that it helps us avoid thinking that we deserve such things, and helps us avoid being disappointed when we don't get them. One of Jesus' main points in the immediate context is that we have no reason to worry; concentrating on the right things helps us not to. There is no reason to add to our troubles by worrying.

April 2
Love and Truth

LOVE AND TRUTH GO together. Among other things, both are unselfish. God loved Israel (Deut 7:7–8) and the world (John 3:16) not because of what they were or what they could do for him, but because he loved them/us. It seems that love and truth are often confused. Love is often equated with a good feeling. If one hears the truth and they don't like it, they naturally assume that there is a lack of love. Paul taught that truth is foundational to the Christian life, and that love governs truth. Love rejoices in the truth (1 Cor 13:6), and Christians are to be speaking truth in love (Eph 4:15). The truth is upheld by the church (1 Tim 3:15); love is a characteristic that qualifies truth.

April 3
"Please Come"

THE PROCESS OF FORGIVENESS begins in the mind. In the mind is where we hear the gospel (Rom 10:14), are thereby pricked in our heart (Acts 2:37), and are thus led to repent (Acts 2:38; the Greek word translated "repent" literally means an "after-mind"). Thus God invited Israel: "Please come, so that we may resolve (this), says the LORD; even though your sins are as crimson, they will be (made) white as snow. Even though they be red as scarlet, they will be as wool" (Isa 1:18). The Hebrew word translated "resolve (this)" in this verse has a meaning of arguing. We decide to come to God, which will then lead us to the point of discussion. God's invitation to argue also suggests that he is willing to hear our side of the story (God asked Adam whether he ate the fruit, Gen 3:11). Forgiveness is what God wants for us. Thus he tells us, "Please come."

April 4

"Have This Mind"

PAUL'S WORDS IN PHIL 2:5 remind us of the choice we have with regard to where our thoughts are centered: "have this mind among yourselves, which is yours in Christ Jesus" (Phil 2:5). One of the great things about the mind is that we can choose what goes into it and on what it dwells. So in the Bible the Christian is taught that they can't set their mind on things both spiritual and things earthly, and that one's mind must be set on one or the other (Rom 8:5). We therefore must choose, on a daily basis, on what we concentrate. Do we concentrate, for example, on the One who will provide for us rather than on provisions; or on how a bad situation can affect our soul, rather than the problem itself? Of course we must think about such things as how to solve problems. But as Christians the primary focus of our thoughts should be on the spiritual rather than the physical. This is the kind of mind the Christian chooses.

April 5
"I Lift My Soul"

THE PSALMIST STATED THAT he lifts his soul to God: "To you, O LORD, I lift my soul" (Ps 25:1). To "lift the soul" has the meaning of directing one's desire. In Ps 24:4, the one who will stand in God's holy place is the one who, among other things, "does not lift his soul to falsehood" (Ps 24:4). This again reminds us that desiring to follow God amounts to a choice. Desires for certain earthly things may or may not be wrong; but pleasure is temporary and should not be the goal of life (1 Tim 5:6). To take "delight" in God and his word (Pss 1:2; 37:4) is rather a spiritual effort, whereby we make the decision to pursue God. Whether it be worship, work, or other aspects of life, the Christian follows God because they choose to; they lift their soul to him, with the promise that God will in turn incline toward them (Jas 4:8).

April 6

How to Set Our Mind

WHAT IS IT TO "set your minds on things that are above, not on things that are on earth" (Col 3:2)? In other words, how do we do that? Paul goes on in Col 3 to explain how one is to live their life as a Christian (Col 3:5—4:6). To put these things into practice begins with looking at life spiritually. This can include such things as adopting an attitude of trying to give God glory rather than satisfying ourselves; when we are faced with a problem, of trying to recall a verse of Scripture (Ps 119:50); and when we are tempted, of using Scripture to combat it (Matt 4:4; Eph 6:17). So setting our mind may not fix our physical problems, but will likely help us become strong in our spiritual lives by focusing on heaven rather than earth and will therefore make life better.

April 7

God's Got This

In Josh 1 Israel was preparing to enter the land that God had promised to give them. Yet this chapter speaks of it as a land that God "is giving" to them (v. 2), which God "had given" to them (v. 3), and which God "will give" to them (v. 13; see also the ESV). How can all three tenses ("giving," "had given," and "will give") be true? Faith means that God, in combination with our doing our part (Jas 2:24–26), is in process of making something happen; that God has already taken care of it (Mark 11:24); and that the result may be yet to be realized. Our part is to accept and hold onto this "threefold cord," never letting go of the fact that God will see to it—no matter what the outcome is.

April 8

"Remember the Word"

ANOTHER KEY ASPECT OF Israel's inheriting the promised land (see yesterday's "Daily") is found in Josh 1:13: "remember the word which Moses the servant of the LORD commanded you, as follows: 'the LORD your God is giving you rest, and thus he will give you this land.'" The word "remember" again can mean to give attention to, as well as to call to mind. After being told to remember, Moses goes on to say "and thus he will give . . . ." For God to give them the promised land depended on their keeping his word. As Christians, our entering the promised land of heaven depends on our keeping his word today (Rev 20:4).

April 9

Spiritual Success

As Joshua prepared to lead the nation into the promised land, in Josh 1:8 he was told, "This book of the instruction is not to depart from your mouth; but you are to meditate thereon day and night." While the verse goes on to include several promises that are part of this injunction, Joshua's part is to make God's word the whole of his speech (his mouth) and his thoughts (upon what he is to meditate). The promise of Joshua's evidently physical success in battle (also v. 8) depended on his spiritual diligence, that is, of keeping God's word. Christians in the same way are to take up the "sword of the Spirit" (Eph 6:11–17) so that we can be successful—not necessarily to get life to work, but to win the spiritual battle in which we are called to engage. If we concentrate on God's word and use it in our lives we will be spiritually successful.

April 10

"Praise the Lord"

INASMUCH AS IT IS a songbook, one of the purposes of the book of Psalms is to praise the Lord. Psalms 146–50 all begin and end with the words "praise the LORD." This phrase consists of two words in Hebrew, elsewhere expressed in English with the word *hallelujah*. In the psalms this word is in the form of a command. Other verses in these chapters contain an invitation to praise with more of an expression of the will ("let them praise," 148:5, 13, etc.). Why are we commanded to do something that is good for us and that can be enjoyable? Perhaps because we won't naturally do it; perhaps because otherwise we won't stop what we're doing to direct our focus away from ourselves; or perhaps because, like most other things that are good for us, it requires more effort. In the NT we are told to sing, among other things, "psalms" (Eph 5:19). We are directed to sing a genre wherein we are commanded to praise the Lord. What better way to engage our thoughts than by complying with God's desire for what is best for us—praising him.

April 11

"Our Daily Bread"

WHEN JESUS TAUGHT US to pray "give us this day our daily bread" (Matt 6:11) it reminds us of the need to not worry about storing up for the future. Not that storing up is necessarily wrong; but it can produce a spiritual disadvantage if we place our hope in our savings. Along these same lines, Jesus also said, "So is the one who lays up treasure for himself and is not rich toward God" (Luke 12:21). Savings can be very practical when the need arises; a key to preserving a proper attitude is rather Jesus' words of being rich toward God. By laying up for ourselves treasures in heaven (Matt 6:20) our heart can be stronger by being settled on the One who should control the money, rather than on uncertain riches (1 Tim 6:17). Savings are not wrong; but being content with food and covering (1 Tim 6:8), or asking for "daily bread" can help us keep our mind and heart rich toward God.

April 12

Controlling Our Thoughts

Is it possible to control our thoughts? Whether it be because of a search engine, news website, social media, or our own mind, there is a reason humans think, and therefore act, the way they do. The Bible teaches us of the importance of such things as consistent input of good things (Phil 4:8, "think on these things") and of the importance of renewing our mind (Rom 12:2). When Paul said that love "taketh not account of evil" (1 Cor 13:5 ASV), the Greek word translated "take account of" is the same as the word translated "think" in Phil 4:8. It has a meaning of adding something to our mind. Rather than denying the existence of evil, this rather tells us of the pervasiveness of evil and that, if we don't choose to take account of the positive, we will likely be dwelling on the negative. Something can control our thoughts, and that something is our mind. "Have this mind in you" (Phil 2:5).

April 13

Keep Going

THE ABILITY TO STAY with a thing, or be persistent, is important for many reasons. One of the main reasons is that the Bible tells us to be. Success in many endeavors usually depends on the ability to keep going, even when one doesn't feel like it. Consistency is important for spiritual reasons, as it demonstrates such things as one's belief in the endeavor to which they are committed. Thus Paul taught "therefore, my beloved brothers, be steadfast, immovable, always abounding in the work of the Lord, knowing that in the Lord your labor is not in vain" (1 Cor 15:58). Sickness and storms are going to happen; yet it is possible to develop the spiritual strength necessary to keep going in spite of such things. The one avenue Paul gives in this verse is for us to remind ourselves that our efforts in the Lord are not for nothing. We may be tempted to quit because our efforts don't seem to be doing any practical good; a reminder to ourselves "that in the Lord your labor is not in vain" can help us to keep going when we perhaps don't feel like it. It can help us be persistent.

April 14

Casting on God

SOME THINGS DETRIMENTAL TO our soul must be dealt with simply by getting rid of them (for example, "let all bitterness and wrath and anger and clamor and slander be put away from you, along with all malice," Eph 4:31). Along the same lines, Peter taught "casting all your anxieties on him, because He cares for you" (1 Pet 5:7). The word *cast* suggests that anxieties are a burden too heavy for us to bear, and must therefore be thrown aside. The Greek word so translated is the same as in Luke 19:35, where the disciples cast their garments onto the colt ridden by Jesus. We need not be burdened with anxieties. The best way to deal with them is to heed the words of Peter and cast them onto God to carry for us, lest they be detrimental to our soul.

April 15

"It Is Good to Praise God"

IN PS 147:1, THE charge to praise the Lord is accompanied by three words that tell us of the spiritual nature of worship: "Praise the LORD! Because it is good to praise God in song; because it is pleasant, and praise is suitable." It is a good thing to unselfishly express our love and appreciation to the Creator of the universe through the spiritual acts of worship. It can be "pleasant" to express our adoration to him if the acts of worship are in harmony with our soul. The fact that worship is "suitable" suggests that it is fitting to the one who desires to be right with God ("a song of praise is suitable to the upright," Ps 33:1). To worship God is good, pleasant, and suitable. Is it therefore the opposite of these three things to not worship God?

April 16

Strength in Weakness

STRENGTH CAN BE ACHIEVED in spite of the weaknesses of the flesh (2 Cor 4:16); and power can rest on us in spite of weaknesses. When Paul spoke of glorying in his weaknesses (referring to his own "thorn in the flesh"), he said that this was for a purpose: "but he said to me, 'My grace is sufficient for you, for my power is made perfect in weakness.' Therefore I will boast all the more gladly of my weaknesses, so that the power of Christ may rest upon me" (2 Cor 12:9). In Paul's example the first key to unlocking this power is his boasting of his weaknesses. Boasting can be a negative thing (Rom 2:23) or a positive thing (Rom 5:11). This boasting can be beneficial for several reasons, including that it focuses attention away from our selfish desires, even if it is a desire to dispense with something unpleasant. Rather than going through life constantly longing for things we think will make us happy, we can rather use negative things to cause us to focus on, and therefore tap into, spiritual things that give us power.

April 17
"Boast More Gladly"

When Paul stated that he would "boast all the more gladly of my weaknesses" (2 Cor 12:9), he was providing for us his second key to unlocking the power of Christ, which is one's attitude. It seems we usually like to boast of things that we take pleasure in, such as some success we have achieved in life. To boast of a weakness or problem could require a change in attitude. The Greek word translated "gladly" in this verse is in a superlative form in Greek, and is accompanied by the word translated "all the more." It is therefore a very strong expression (it would be like saying "more best" in English). Such an attitude can be adopted only if one chooses to. When we have some problem or deficiency in life (see v. 10), again instead of focusing on wishing that it would go away so we could be physically happy, we can rather take delight in it because of what it could mean spiritually. A physical weakness can therefore be the means by which we derive spiritual power from Christ.

April 18

The Goal of Strength

HAVING SPIRITUAL POWER FROM God can and should be a goal for Christians. God told Paul in 2 Cor 12:9, "For my power is made perfect in weakness." The Greek word translated "perfect" has to do with reaching a goal. Paul's third key in this verse was his motivation of reaching the goal of the power of Christ. Paul boasted in his weaknesses "so that the power of Christ may rest upon me." Good can come through hardships if we look past the physical pain to the spiritual goal of having the power of Christ rest upon us. With the right perspective, weakness can be the means of achieving this goal. This was why Paul boasted in his weaknesses, knowing that the end result was something he might not have otherwise. Paul could then be content with his troubles (v. 10), knowing that weaknesses were a key to achieving the goal of strength.

April 19

The Way We Walk

THE WAY WE ARE to live as Christians is often described in the Bible with the word *walk*. In Gal 5:16 Paul said to "walk by the Spirit." This means, or at least includes, living our lives according to the Bible. Paul taught similarly in Col 2:6–7; he states that "as you received Christ Jesus the Lord, so walk in him . . . just as you were taught" (Col 2:6–7). To live "by the Spirit" includes such things as making decisions, overcoming destructive emotions such as anger or worry, and overcoming difficult situations by recalling and applying Scripture. "When we walk with the Lord in the light of his word," we will be living a spiritual life, inasmuch as it will be walking "by the Spirit."

April 20

Seeing Is Believing

MOST OF US TEND to believe what we see and to question what we hear (do you believe me?). This can make it more difficult to believe the Bible, because many times we form conclusions based on what we see; and when our beliefs seem to not match the Bible, we choose to believe our own conclusions. Jesus' words in John 3:12 show us several things regarding belief: "if I have told you earthly things and you do not believe, how can you believe if I tell you heavenly things?" Jesus often began his teaching by pointing out things we can see (for example, his illustrations from nature regarding birds [Matt 6:26] and flowers [Matt 6:28]). If one won't believe Jesus' teaching on such things, how can they believe his teaching on things pertaining to heaven? God has given us enough evidence that we can believe (Rom 1:20). Why question it?

April 21

Follow the Good

THE CONCEPTS OF GOOD and evil are real. God has defined them for us in the Bible ("it was good," Gen 1:10), so they don't depend on what we think about them. The world tries to redefine good and evil (Isa 5:20), to make them the opposite as presented in the Bible. Thus Ps 1:1–2 speaks of these two possible life paths: "Blessed is the one who does not walk by the advice of (the) wicked, nor stand in the way of (the) sinners, nor sit in the seat of (the) scornful. But his delight is in the LORD's instruction, and he meditates on His instruction day and night." Living a life pleasing to God begins with choosing the right way. To search and follow the good is also based on our desire for truth. The life we live often shows itself (Jesus said, "You will recognize them by their fruits," Matt 7:16). A right life begins with the path we choose and continues by walking along this path to the end, walking in the way that is good.

April 22

Preaching as an Act of Worship

WORSHIP FOR THE CHRISTIAN today includes not only such obvious acts as prayer (1 Tim 2:8) and singing (Col 3:16), but also preaching as an act of worship. In Matt 15:9 Jesus (quoting Isaiah) referred to teaching as an act of worship: "in vain do they worship me, teaching as doctrines the commandments of men." Teaching, in the form of preaching today, is no less an act of corporate worship. While worship by definition is something that is directed toward God, preaching is an activity that flows from God to us (as it is the extension of his written word to our ears through the medium of the preacher, 1 Pet 4:11). While the implications of this for both preacher and listener are many, this fundamental fact can help us to focus on this phase of worship in order to make our engagement therein pleasing to God. Among other things, maintaining this thought can help with regard to other things such as the entertainment or the comfort factor. Rather, when we gather together "as one man" (Neh 8:1), we may be so moved by the fact that God is speaking to us that we act as the congregation in Neh 8:5: "Then Ezra opened the book in full view of all the people, because he was above all the people, and as he opened it all the people stood." Not that we must do this; but if our heart is not right with regard to all of worship, we might be offering it in vain.

April 23
A Purpose of Rest

ALTHOUGH REST IS PLEASURABLE, it also serves a practical purpose, in that it is the time (not, for example, while we're jogging) that we become stronger. This suggests that one reason we rest is so that we can gain strength to return to our activity. Rest is one of the first concepts we read about in the Bible (Gen 2:3), and it is upheld later by God in the law of Moses (Exod 20:8–10). As Christians we have work to do (1 Cor 15:58); we rest today, among other things, so that we can keep doing our work. One day we will enjoy an eternal rest, not so that we can return to our labor, but as a pleasurable eternal reward for a life of labor in the Lord (Rev 14:13).

April 24

"How Majestic Is God's Name"

THE PSALMIST STATED, "O LORD, our Lord, how majestic is your name in all the earth! You who have set your splendor upon the heavens" (Ps 8:1). The psalmist praises God by praising his name. Jesus taught similarly when he gave the model prayer in Matt 6, beginning with the words "hallowed be thy name" (v. 9, ASV). How we treat God's name is a reflection of our reverence or lack thereof toward him; his name stands for him. The Ten Commandments state that an Israelite was not to take the name of the Lord in vain (Exod 20:7). When one is converted today they are baptized into the name of Christ. This is, or is part of, calling on his name (Rom 10:13). So it is fitting to praise God, not just by stating his name (Matt 7:21), but by exclaiming that God's name, or he himself, is majestic in all the earth.

April 25

Memories and Moments

JAMES SAID THAT LIFE is temporary: "Yet you do not know what tomorrow will bring. What is your life? For you are a mist that appears for a little time and then vanishes" (Jas 4:14). Whether they are precious or painful, memories are in the past and can be forgotten (Phil 3:13), and moments, whether precious or painful, are not lasting. The most important thing, therefore, is that which is spiritual. Naturally we have to give attention to such things as problems. But problems will pass; and the beautiful day we wish would never end will end. Neither one therefore should devastate our soul. When our focus is on heaven (Col 3:2) and things spiritual (Matt 6:33), the temporary things take on less importance. Focusing on the spiritual gives us a joy that rises above any memory or moment, whether precious or painful.

April 26
When Good Things Happen

WHAT IS OUR REACTION when "good" things happen? As with anything out of the ordinary, whether "good" or "bad," our reaction depends on our heart. Peter's reaction to the catch of fish in Luke 5 teaches us a lot regarding spiritual things. After they had worked all night, Jesus told Peter to throw out his nets, which resulted in an extraordinary catch of fish (vv. 4–7). Peter's reaction was that "he fell down at Jesus' knees, saying, 'Depart from me, for I am a sinful man, O Lord'" (Luke 5:8). This is a reflection of Rom 2:4, "God's kindness is meant to lead you to repentance." Surely there is nothing wrong with delighting in good things. But the ultimate purpose of things in life, whether "good" or "bad," can be to cause us to look to God. If we ask for good things, either for ourselves or others, it is good to pause and remember why we ask—that such can direct our heart toward God, ultimately so that his will be done (Jas 4:15).

April 27

Anger, but No Worries

WHY DOES THE BIBLE say that the Christian can be angry (Eph 4:26) but they cannot be anxious (or worry, Phil 4:6)? Perhaps because anger may be a more difficult emotion to overcome than anxiety? Perhaps because worry involves the thoughts more than anger? Ephesians 4:26 states that one can be angry as long as it doesn't cause them to sin: "Be angry and do not sin; do not let the sun go down on your anger." Since worry has to do with fear, and fear is the opposite of faith (see Matt 14:28–30; Rev 21:8) this means it is likely impossible to worry and trust God at the same time. One can perhaps be (temporarily) angry with God, but a lack of faith (as manifested through fear or worry) is unacceptable to him (Heb 11:6). Anger can be overcome by putting it away (Eph 4:31); fear must be overcome with faith. We maintain faith to overcome our fears and to avoid God being angry with us.

April 28

The Debt of Sin

To be in debt is not necessarily sinful, but to be in sin is to be in debt. Sin is an obligation that must be paid back. The trouble is that, unlike financial debt, sin is a violation that can't be paid back by sinners, and the consequences of not paying it back are much more serious. For this reason (ironically) the One who is owed this debt has provided a way for the debtor to be forgiven. Again, redemption means acceptance of the terms of forgiveness, and Jesus' death is the means of redemption; he paid the price for our sins. Thus Paul said, "in him we have redemption through his blood, the forgiveness of our trespasses, according to the riches of his grace" (Eph 1:7). It is an irony of ironies that it is through God's grace that he has provided a means for us to be forgiven of the debt we owe him, without which we would remain in debt to him, because we would thereby remain in sin.

April 29
"The Heavens Declare the Glory of God"

THERE IS NOT A much more glorious thing to behold than the sky and all it contains, especially during transitional times of the year. The heavens have a type of glory; the heavenly bodies radiate an eminence that has arrested the attention of humans throughout their existence, even to the point of humans desiring to worship them. Yet, for all of their wondrous beauty, these things attest to the glory of the Creator who placed them there. Psalm 19:1 states, "The heavens recount the glory of God, and the expanse declares the work of his hands." This statement carries the force of logic: If the sky is glorious, how much more is the glory of the Creator who placed them there? Any physical wonder is a reflection of the spiritual Being behind their existence (Rom 1:20); they declare the glory of God and therefore should cause us to want to glorify him.

April 30

Understanding Scripture

UNDERSTANDING SCRIPTURE CAN BE both a process and a goal. That is, Scripture not being a manual with explicit instructions on how to get life to work means that sometimes it may not be clear, but that its clarity may be revealed as life proceeds. John 2:22 reads, "When therefore he was raised from the dead, his disciples remembered that he had said this, and they believed the Scripture and the word that Jesus had spoken." The disciples remembered Jesus' words. This happened in part because they had Jesus' words in their head and evidently held onto them. There may be times in life when Scripture doesn't make complete sense at the moment, yet this is no reason to assume that it is untrue. Instead of discarding it, we should rather store it in our heart (Ps 119:11) in view of it one day making sense. Keeping God's word is our process; remembering it in view of moments of clarity is to be one of our goals.

May 1

May Day

THE DISTRESS SIGNAL THAT sounds like "May Day" is actually a French phrase (*m'aidez*) meaning "help me." There are always times in life when we will need help. It was not good for man to be alone; thus God made a "helper" suitable for him (Gen 2:18). As Christians the Lord is our "helper" (Ps 54:4). When we have heavy burdens to lift, we have help for the task. The Holy Spirit helps our prayers rise to heaven (Rom 8:26), and our brethren help us with burdens in this life (Gal 6:2). We are not alone.

May 2
Giving God Our Will

ONE OF THE MOST important things we can give God is our will. It is not necessarily wrong to want things (Ps 37:4); but even legitimate desires are best left to God's will. Though the reasons for this can be many, to receive the things for which we long is usually ultimately not satisfying. More importantly, to condition our heart toward God's is an expression of our desire to please him. In other words, giving our heart over to him is in effect an expression of love. Paul said that love "does not insist on its own way" (1 Cor 13:5); that is, love is basically unselfish. If we submit to God's will, like Jesus in the garden (Mark 14:36), it shows God we love him. A key therefore to fulfilling this aspect of a relationship with God is to always include in our requests "thy will be done." By giving God our will we give up ourselves, because it shows we believe him when we read in his word that "love does not insist on its own way."

May 3
"I Press On"

WHEN LIFE IS DIFFICULT, as it is going to be, what reason does one have to keep going? Especially for the non-Christian, what is the motivation for continuing to try in this life? Perhaps it is such things as making money, or the support of family and friends, which are not necessarily wrong. But what if one didn't have those things; or what if those things didn't last, as they are not going to (even the best of friends can't attend one another's funerals)? The Christian has a motivation for pressing on that will not go away. Paul said, "I press on toward the goal for the prize of the upward call of God in Christ Jesus" (Phil 3:14). Paul's motivation in this verse is something that is not physical. Again, not that it is necessarily wrong to be motivated by other things; but what a blessing it is for the Christian to know that their motivation is based on an eternal goal. The difficulties of life therefore need not stop the Christian from pressing on toward the ultimate goal of eternal life.

May 4

In Spite of This

ONE WAY TO DEVELOP faith is to overcome fear. It seems we often don't want to think of "what's the worst that could happen," evidently because this produces fear. Yet contemplating a fear can be the means to help us overcome it with faith. The psalmist said, "If an army should encamp next to me, my heart will not fear; if a war should arise against me, in spite of this I trust" (Ps 27:3). Just as in Ps 23:4 ("even though I should walk through the valley of the shadow of death"), twice he states that even if something negative should happen, he would not be afraid, and he would even "trust." The psalmist pictured the worst that could happen, and then overcame it with faith. To be fearful is not good (Rev 21:8); to imagine a fearful thing can serve the purpose of helping us develop faith by overcoming our fear.

May 5

Worshiping Together

THE PSALMIST IN PS 34:3 offers a call to collective worship: "Magnify the LORD with me, so that we may exalt his name together!" (Ps 34:3). The first word "magnify" is a command, meaning "cause the Lord to be great." The second is more of an invitation, in the sense of "don't you think we should exalt his name?" While the actions to which the psalmist calls us are good, the other two aspects of this verse remind us of one of the main blessings of worship, that it is carried out together (from the psalmist's words "with me," and "together"). Some aspects of worship today can be carried out anywhere. Some, such as singing one to another and communion, are to be carried out together. In what other way can we be so edified, than by magnifying God and exalting his name with others of a like, precious faith? Not to mention that Jesus is together with us when we do (Matt 18:20).

May 6

"In My Prosperity"

ONE OF THE GREATEST dangers of wealth is what it does to the soul. One can maintain a proper attitude while being wealthy, though the Bible teaches that riches make it very difficult to keep one's mind focused on God. The psalmist stated, "And as for me, I said in my prosperity, 'I will never be moved'" (Ps 30:6). One of the keys in this verse is the phrase "in my prosperity." It is not necessarily wrong to be wealthy, and it is good to be confident with regard to such things as God controlling the future (Jas 4:13–15). The psalmist evidently placed all of his trust in his prosperity, rather than having an attitude such as expressed in Job 1:21, "The LORD has given, and the LORD has taken away; blessed be the name of the LORD." Prosperity is not really the point here; in the psalmist's case it was the attitude adopted in prosperity of which one needs to be cautious. The Christian can learn how to prosper (Phil 4:11–12), by having their heart centered on the treasure of spiritual things (Matt 6:21). With the right heart, nothing need remove the Christian's spiritual life, including prosperity.

May 7

What Will People Think?

To what extent should we be concerned about what others think? On the one hand it is good to be aware of such things as the Christian's influence among those around him (Paul said, "I have become all things to all people, that by all means I might save some," 1 Cor 9:22). On the other hand others' opinions should not be the Christian's first concern. Such verses as Jesus' warning, "woe to you, when all people speak well of you" (Luke 6:26), and the apostles' statement that "we must obey God rather than men" (Acts 5:29), remind us that there is a higher standard than what others think. If the Christian loves "the glory that comes from man more than the glory that comes from God" (John 12:43), the day may come when they will deny the Lord out of this very concern (Matt 10:33). Woe unto them if they do.

May 8

"The Peace of God"

WE SPEAK OF THE concept of peace in life in many ways, including such things as a cease-fire during time of war. The biblical concept of peace, a blessing given to the Christian, is a quality different from the worldly understanding thereof, because it is a quality that comes from God. Jesus said, "Peace I leave with you; my peace I give to you. Not as the world gives do I give to you" (John 14:27a). The quality of peace is a spiritual quality because it comes from God (the "peace of God," Phil 4:7), and is the result of living a spiritual life (part of the "fruit of the Spirit," Gal 5:22). While a type of peace can seemingly be attained in this life by pursuing calm and tranquility in different ways, true peace can only come by availing oneself of this spiritual quality that comes from the God of peace (Phil 4:9). The Christian has peace because their spiritual life is right with this God (Rom 5:1).

May 9

Got You Covered

SOMETHING THAT CONSISTS OF several different parts, like a house with several rooms but no roof, can be unified by being given something as simple as a covering. Sin makes God unhappy with us and separates us from him (Isa 59:2; Eph 2:12) and from each other (Eph 2:14). Sin can't be compensated for by anything we do of our own (Eph 2:8–9). In the OT, the Hebrew word translated "atone" has a dual meaning of both appeasing and covering. To have our sins covered, today by the blood of Christ, pacifies the heart of God so that he is no longer unhappy with us. And thus having our sins covered makes us to be atoned, or "at one'" with him and with each other.

May 10

"I Will Sing Praise"

Do you plan to go to worship on the first day of the week? Do you plan what you are going to do when you get there? The psalmist said, "Let me give thanks (to) the Lord with all my heart; let me recount all your wondrous works. Let me rejoice and exult in you; let me sing praise to your name, O Most High" (Ps 9:1–2). Though he didn't say when or under what circumstances he would do these things, he nevertheless expressed four means by which he would worship God. Whatever benefit we derive from corporate worship is ultimately due to the fact that worship is unselfish. Preparing for such things as the hardships of life (1 Pet 1:13) or an aspect of worship such as giving (1 Cor 16:2) can help condition our heart, and, in the case of worship, thereby make it more beneficial to us. It can do this because we are thereby participating in worship with regard to one of its primary purposes, to bring glory to God.

May 11

"How Can You Believe"

A SEARCH FOR TRUTH that begins with the belief that God's word is truth (John 17:17), and that does not quit, should lead us to Jesus. The people Jesus addressed in John 5 claimed to believe the Scriptures; yet Jesus' words suggest that they would never come to believe in him, even though they constantly searched the Scriptures (John 5:39). Jesus said, "How can you believe, when you receive glory from one another and do not seek the glory that comes from the only God?" (John 5:44); and "for if you believed Moses, you would believe me; for he wrote of me. But if you do not believe his writings, how will you believe my words?" (John 5:46–47). They had set their hope on Moses (v. 45), evidently rather than setting their hope or basing their search on truth. If they had set their hope on and pursued the truth, with a dash of logic, their search would have led them to Jesus. To engage in such a pursuit means that we can find the truth (Matt 7:8), and thus not have to hear Jesus say we can't believe in him.

May 12
Doing the Right Thing

DOING THE RIGHT THING means one's actions are based on a standard. To live this way includes the idea that one does what they do whether it means they receive an immediate reward for their actions or not. Jesus said, "And if you do good to those who do good to you, what benefit is that to you? For even sinners do the same" (Luke 6:33). To expect a reward betrays a possible selfish motivation of the heart and will likely lead to discouragement if a reward is not forthcoming. To believe in a standard means such things as worshiping God regardless of any repercussions (Dan 3:18), preaching the gospel no matter what may result (Acts 14:19), and resisting temptation whether it improves their life or not. The Christian does the right thing because they follow a standard of right and wrong; and they will one day be rewarded for their efforts (Rev 21:7).

May 13

The Lord Alone

One of the times in daily life when we are the most vulnerable is when we are asleep. While we can fix and control many things of a physical nature, we can do none of these when we are asleep. Our attitude in this regard betrays wherein our heart is truly centered and upon what we truly depend. The psalmist stated, "In peace I will both lie down and sleep; for you alone, O Lord, you have me dwell in safety" (Ps 4:8). He can sleep well, being both in peace and in safety, because of God. One of the keys to gathering meaning from this verse is the word "alone." The psalmist describes in poetic language his reliance on God. We can do many things, and get life to work, by effort and focus. Where do we go when we are vulnerable (and thus also when we are not)? Should it not be to the Lord—"alone"?

May 14

Overcome Evil

EVIL IS A POWERFUL force. It has a tendency to permeate (Gal 5:9) and can overcome the Christian (Rom 12:21). The Bible therefore teaches Christians of their need to resist evil. The Christian is to overcome evil by doing good, to resist the devil (Jas 4:7), and to look for and take the way out of temptation (1 Cor 10:13). As with almost anything good, all of these require effort, and therefore require strength (Eph 6:10). If we put effort into gaining spiritual strength by applying ourselves to prayer, knowledge (study) of Scripture, and putting these things into practice (Heb 5:14), we will be better equipped to overcome evil. The effort we put into gaining this strength will give us a strength powerful enough to overcome the forces of evil. "He who is in you is greater than he who is in the world" (1 John 4:4).

May 15

"Give Ear to My Prayer, O God"

WE SHOULD FEEL HONORED to be able to worship God. Listening can be hard work and is an unselfish action when borne of a desire to help the one speaking. It is a good thing that the Lord is always willing to listen; his ear is not heavy (Isa 59:1). Thus the psalmist pleaded with God in Ps 55 to listen to him: "Give ear, O God, to my prayer, and do not hide yourself from my appeal" (Ps 55:1). God doesn't have to listen to us; yet he always does (Deut 4:7). If we adopt an attitude that prayer and other aspects of worship are a privilege, it could contribute to worship always being a joy in which to engage. God wants us to come to him (Heb 4:16); should we not want to?

May 16
"Like a Tree"

GOD'S WORD OFFERS MANY answers to life's most basic questions from a spiritual basis. To concentrate on God's word in our daily life gives us a stability that we can get in no other way. The book of psalms begins by stating that the godly one meditates on God's word day and night (Ps 1:2), with the result that "thus he will be like a tree planted by channels of waters" (Ps 1:3). This description as well as what follows provides many positive images, including that trees are stable, and that they don't grow to maturity immediately. Just as the benefit of other good habits such as diet and exercise are often not noticed immediately, so concentrating on God's word may help us today; but it also gives us stability like a planted tree, something that we may realize tomorrow.

May 17

"You Are Seeking Me"

ONE CAN SEEK JESUS for different reasons. Jesus said to the multitude, "Truly, truly, I say to you, you are seeking me, not because you saw signs, but because you ate your fill of the loaves" (John 6:26). Two choices involved in Jesus' description included seeking Jesus for the physical versus the spiritual, and seeking him for selfish versus unselfish reasons. It is natural to want to be fed when one is hungry. Though they do not occur today, a biblical "sign" is a miracle that points the observer to something else. To seek Jesus for spiritual reasons is to pursue a life that desires to bring glory to him, as one focuses on heaven and on spiritual things. In process thereof, and as a result of their being unselfish, God provides their needs such as food (Phil 4:19).

May 18

"Think about These Things"—Again

To return to Phil 4:8, Paul said, "Finally, brothers, whatever is true, whatever is honorable, whatever is just, whatever is pure, whatever is lovely, whatever is commendable, if there is any excellence, if there is anything worthy of praise, think about these things." Again, to "think" in this verse is to take account of in the mind. How does one do that? Often the negative aspects of life seem to dominate and to recur in our minds. That is, it seems that it takes more effort, and more consistent effort, to harbor positive thoughts. The word Paul uses for "think" is in a form that has two important senses. One is that it is an imperative, or command form, telling us of the necessity of following this teaching. The other is that the word has a sense of doing repeatedly. To consistently take account of God's word, through reading, recall (that is, repeating it to oneself), or audibly, can do many things for our soul, including keeping the negative thoughts from recurring, as well as feeding our soul with the spiritual power it needs.

May 19

"Whatever Is True"

CONTINUING WITH PHIL 4:8 (see yesterday's "Daily"), how can we conclude from this verse that it is Scripture that is to be the primary thoughts we add to our mind? The things we think about throughout our day might be nice thoughts that make us feel good, but are not directly from Scripture. It seems that Paul's teaching in Phil 4:8 is that which we are to be adding to the account of our mind ultimately should be based on God's word. For example, that which is "lovely" to one person may be a meadow with flowers, while to another it may be running in the chilly rain. Perhaps this is why Paul begins his list with the word "true." God's word is truth (John 17:17). Not that we can't think on something besides God's word; but when engaged in mental exercise either to help our soul, to help us mentally deal with particular situations, or in the hope of gaining wisdom to figure out life, it is good if God's word is the basis of our thoughts. "The instruction of the LORD is perfect, restoring the soul; the testimony of the LORD is verified, making wise the simple" (Ps 19:7).

May 20
Giving Based on the Past and the Future

GIVING AS AN ACT of worship is to be based on both the past and the future. It is based on the past, as Paul said the Christian is to give "as he may prosper" (1 Cor 16:2). While God surely appreciates sacrificial giving (2 Cor 8:2–3), we are to make our decision on the amount to give based on our level of prosperity. Our giving is also to be based on the future, That is, when contemplating both the act as well as the amount of giving, Christians can recall verses that speak of God's response, that he will give back to us accordingly (Luke 6:38; 2 Cor 9:6–11). Both of these principles remind us that giving as an act of worship is to be viewed financially, based on our prosperity, as well as spiritually; that is, by doing such things as contemplating Bible verses, as well as praying that our giving is acceptable to God. By so doing we can use giving as a means of glorifying the God who promised he will see to our needs, rather than looking at it as a financial transaction.

May 21

"My Ways"

ONE REASON IT IS good for us to leave the outcome of our prayers up to God is because God does not act the way we do. God's ways are higher than ours (Isa 55:8–9); and there is a way which seems right to man (Prov 14:12), though it may not be. Our approach to problems is often the opposite of what God instructs us to do. For example, our solution to financial problems may be to get more money, while with God we are admonished "give and it will be given to you" (Luke 6:38). Our desire for greatness is attained by doing great things, while God's path to greatness is through humility (1 Pet 5:6). The common element in all of these factors is an emphasis on the spiritual rather than the physical (John 6:63). We may receive what we ask for when we pray; but the more important thing is such spiritual aspects as our conforming our will to his and, in process of asking and of doing, that we will become more like God (1 John 3:2).

May 22

Untouchable Joy

CIRCUMSTANCES MAY CONTRIBUTE TO the Christian's happiness, but they do not determine his or her joy (Gal 5:22). With God watching over us, all is right with the world. God watches over everyone in a general way (Matt 5:45), and he watches over his children in particular (Rom 8:28). We provoke trouble inside ourselves with worry, and there are always dangers from outside (Ps 91:5). A key to overcoming that which is on the outside is the strength we nurture inside. Such spiritual enemies as fear and worry may be prompted by outer circumstances. And though these circumstances may be beyond our control, the fear and worry are not. By concentrating our mind on appropriate qualities such as faith, hope, joy, etc., the Christian can lean upon the psalmist's assurances that we need not be afraid (Pss 23:4; 91:5). Even though outward circumstances may be stressful, the child of God has a joy that these circumstances cannot affect (Hab 3:17–18).

May 23

That Which Is Given

ONE OF THE BEST ways to receive help from God is to first give to him. God offers a promise of reciprocation when we do such things as call upon him (Jer 33:3) and give first to him (Luke 6:38). The Christian is invited to cast upon God the worries they invent (1 Pet 5:7); and the psalmist taught to roll our way upon the Lord (Ps 37:5). Both of these have to do with specific negative things that plague our lives. Psalm 55:22 adds an additional promise of sustenance when we cast these upon God: "cast your portion upon the LORD, and he for his part will sustain you. He will never permit the righteous to slip." The Hebrew word translated "cast" suggests an image of carrying something too heavy to be borne. The word translated "portion," however, comes from a Hebrew word meaning "to give" (as something given to us). We might invent worries, and we might have problems in life due to our own choices. The promise of this verse is that of God sustaining us when we give life back to him, whether a heavy burden or not. God wants to support us; first we must turn over to him not just the burdens that weigh us down, but whatever has been given to us.

May 24

Politics and Religion

POLITICS AND RELIGION GO together, inasmuch as political rule can influence the way Christians live and whether they are allowed to worship. Not every country throughout history has allowed its citizens to worship the way they choose. As the first day of the week approaches one may or may not be thinking about either politics or religion. To begin looking forward to worshiping God with others can help us keep all things, including politics, in perspective. The intersection of the spiritual and the political was expressed by the psalmist, who said, "The nations will rejoice and cry out, because You will judge the peoples with equity, and You will guide the nations in the earth" (Ps 67:4). These verses remind us in general of the importance of singing praise to God, an expression of adoration that includes the fact that God is judge of all the earth. Again, who the leader of our country is is important, and Christians are taught to be obedient to their rulers (1 Pet 2:13–14). Yet God is ultimately the judge who will rule with equity (the Hebrew word translated "equity" has to do with "straightness") and who has an overriding providence that rulers cannot affect. The fact that God is ultimately in charge gives Christians a reason to praise him. Freedom and truth go hand in hand. "Will not the judge of all the earth do right?" (Gen 18:25).

May 25
To Do God's Will

ONE REASON TRUTH IS difficult to accept is because it can at times go against our will. While we naturally want to hear things that are pleasing to the ear, truth often makes us uncomfortable, to the point that many have "itching ears" (2 Tim 4:3–4) or a desire to hear some new thing (Acts 17:21) rather than truth. The difficulty of accepting truth can be overcome by developing a heart that desires God's will over ours. Jesus said, "If anyone's will is to do God's will, he will know whether the teaching is from God or whether I am speaking on my own authority" (John 7:17). Jesus' audience claimed to love the law of Moses but were misguided, as they sought to kill Jesus because of his teaching (v. 19). By conditioning our heart to be more like God's (Ps 37:4), we can with such an attitude be better conditioned to accept truth when confronted with it. By the same token, if we hear the truth of Jesus' teaching and we don't like it, what does that say about the condition of our heart or will?

May 26

Jesus Was Verified

IN JOHN 5 ARE three avenues through which Jesus' identity was verified. In v. 33, John the baptizer bore witness of Jesus. In v. 36, Jesus' works bore witness of him; and in v. 39, the word bore witness to Jesus. A seeming reason why Jesus was not and is not accepted by all is not in the witnesses, but in the mind of the hearer. All of the most verifiable evidence will do no good if the heart that it confronts is not willing to accept the truth. That is, accepting that Jesus is who he claimed to be (the Son of God, Messiah) still boils down to accepting truth. One can be shown all of the evidence to the point that it can only be denied if the hearer wants to deny it. Lies are more easily accepted than truth; thus Jesus did all he could to get us to believe in him. What will you do with the evidence; what will you do with Jesus?

May 27

Why Bother?

In Job 21:15, Job in his despair asked, "What is the Almighty, that we should serve him? And what will we profit if we should meet with him?" If we sacrifice time, effort, and emotions, most of us probably would like to see some positive result for so doing. Evil is a constant force that can continue to grow (Gal 5:9). This suggests that there will be times in life when one may have to do the right thing, even though there may not be a noticeable benefit; we don't always see a positive result for doing the right thing (in Luke 15:25–30 the elder brother evidently expected a reward for being a good son). As Christians, we do the right thing, among other things, to unselfishly bring glory to God. To expect something in return could betray a heart inclined toward selfishness. Christians should rather serve God out of love, which is unselfish (John 3:16). Our labor in the Lord "is not in vain" (1 Cor 15:58); that is, it is not for nothing, and therefore it is for something, and therein is the profit.

May 28

Worthless Guys

WHEN ASKING THE QUESTION of wherein lies the profit (see yesterday's "Daily"), we may build upon the question of "for whom is the profit?" by a consideration of Eli's sons Hophni and Phineas. The Bible describes them in 1 Sam 2:12 as not good guys: "Now Eli's sons were worthless guys; they did not know the LORD." The phrase used to describe them is not translated the same across several published translations (ASV, "base men"; ESV, RSV, and NASB, "worthless men"; KJV, "sons of Belial"; NIV, "scoundrels"). The reason given for their being worthless guys is, however, the same in every translation (except the NIV), which is "they did not know the LORD." The phrase "worthless guys" means in Hebrew "one without profit" (it is related to the word so translated in Job 21:15). Not knowing the Lord, or not being in a right relationship with him, makes one a worthless person. The slave Onesimus, whose name means "profitable," had been converted to the Lord after he had run away (see the book of Philemon). He was now truly profitable. Being in a right relationship with God makes one profitable to God. One may be a "good person" under the evaluation of men; but, spiritually speaking, they are of greatest value to God when they are right with him.

May 29

"Let Me Sing of Justice"

THE WRITER OF Ps 101 was evidently bothered by the conduct of his countrymen. He recognized his need to do right (vv. 2–4), while maintaining a distance from those who didn't (v. 3b, 5, 7, 8). He was concerned about those who turned away from the Lord (v. 3b), those whose heart was not right (v. 4), those who slandered and were arrogant (v. 5), etc. In spite of (because of?) the improper behavior of some of his countrymen, the psalmist focused his worship efforts, specifically his songs, on the spiritual concepts of "justice" and "covenant loyalty" (or "lovingkindness," v. 1). Perhaps he did so because he saw these lacking in the land. If so, it seems he focused on these spiritual concepts as motivation to engage in the higher purpose of praising God. Thus he began this psalm (v. 1), not with complaint about the things weighing upon his heart, but in praise to God: "let me sing of covenant loyalty and of justice; to you, O LORD, let me sing praise."

May 30

The Spirit of Marriage

GOD INSTITUTED, AND THEREFORE defined, the relationship of marriage (Gen 2:24). Scripture teaching regarding marriage shows that it is a relationship that is to operate according to spiritual principles. One key to a good marriage is an emphasis on such principles as a husband and wife loving each other (Eph 5:25; Titus 2:4). Likewise, one key to a spiritually strong life is a good marriage. Peter said that a husband needs to focus on a good relationship with his wife for this reason: "Ye husbands, in like manner, dwell with your wives according to knowledge, giving honor unto the woman, as unto the weaker vessel, as being also joint heirs of the grace of life; to the end that your prayers be not hindered" (1 Pet 3:7 ASV). While the benefits of a good marriage are many, the reason Peter offers for concentrating on a having a good relationship with one's wife is for the purpose of a strong spiritual life (that his "prayers be not hindered"). For a husband to concentrate on having a good relationship with his wife helps his prayer life; and a strong prayer life contributes to a good marriage.

May 31

Overcome Evil

THE BIBLE OFFERS THE Christian many responses to the force of evil, including dwelling on the good in one's mind (Phil 4:8), abhorring evil (Rom 12:9), and resisting the devil (Jas 4:7). Paul again stated that evil is a force that can be overcome: "do not be overcome by evil, but overcome evil with good" (Rom 12:21). This verse reminds us of several concepts, including the negative concepts that there is such a thing as evil; that it can be powerful; and that, left alone, it can be a force that can overcome us. The positive concepts contained herein include that good is also a powerful force, that Christians are to overcome evil with good, and that Christians must take the initiative if evil is to be overcome. To not do good, in whatever form good may take, is generally to allow evil to persist and possibly overcome us; and may, on the part of the Christian, be something for which he is held to account before God. "To him therefore that knoweth to do good, and doeth it not, to him it is sin" (Jas 4:17 ASV).

June 1

Remember and Forget

THE PAST IS TO be both remembered and forgotten. The Bible contains many admonitions to remember (Deut 15:15; Luke 16:25; 17:32), and Paul said that he determined to forget the things of the past (Phil 3:13). Both remembering and forgetting are important, and are to be given proper attention, depending upon what we focus. This again reminds us of the proper use of the mind, that it ultimately should be for spiritual purposes. Whether we concentrate on the present (2 Cor 6:2), remember the past (including Jesus' death, 1 Cor 11:24), or forget the past, the common denominator is that we utilize our mind and the appropriate information for our spiritual good.

June 2

"You Ask and Do Not Receive"

Is THERE A PURPOSE to our receiving something for which we pray? While a parent enjoys seeing the happiness in their child after giving them a gift, the parent may also have in mind something deeper they hope to accomplish, that is, a close relationship with their child. When we have a problem or a need, or some unfulfilled desire, we often only want the situation resolved. While this is reasonable, James said that one reason we ask and don't receive is because we ask for the purely selfish reason of being satisfied: "You ask and do not receive, because you ask wrongly, to spend it on your passions" (Jas 4:3). When we do receive something for which we have prayed, a good thing to do is to contemplate the spiritual meaning behind it, that is, such possible implications as what this could mean for our life, whether this can bring us closer to God, make us spiritually stronger, etc., rather than simply our own satisfaction. Jesus said it is more blessed to give than to receive (Acts 20:35); perhaps for this reason God gives us things in response to our requests based on his will, rather than ours (Matt 7:11; 1 John 5:14).

June 3

"Bless the Lord, O My Soul"

IN PS 103:1 THE psalmist stated, "Bless the LORD, O my soul, and all that is within me; (bless) his holy name." The writer commands his soul to bless, or praise the Lord (the Hebrew word usually translated *soul* in the OT often refers simply to the person). When the psalmist commands his soul, it suggests, in poetic language, that he recognizes both the need to direct himself to worship, as well as the implication that he is in charge of his soul. Though humans seem to have an innate desire to worship, the tendency of the natural person seems to be toward the physical rather than the spiritual (1 Cor 2:14). The psalmist recognizes that if he doesn't so direct his soul, his soul may not engage itself in worship. Rather, worship is a spiritual activity one must do themselves. Even though Scripture contains a command and other teaching on worshiping God (Rev 19:10; John 4:24), we still must engage therein ourselves (no one can do it for us). If we don't, as it were, command our soul, we might miss the opportunity to engage in communion with the Creator, and thereby miss an opportunity to strengthen our relationship with him. We are going to serve someone (Matt 6:24); whom will we worship?

June 4

"They Hated Me"

HATRED IS AN EMOTION to be avoided. Yet it seems that some hate for no reason, or misdirect this negative feeling toward the wrong person, usually someone who serves as a lightning rod. Jesus recognized that this was people's attitude toward him, as he quoted Ps 35:19: "But the word that is written in their Law must be fulfilled: 'They hated me without a cause'" (John 15:25). There may be many reasons for hatred arising in the heart. The Christian response to their own hatred can be to overcome it in a positive way, such as choosing to love one's enemies (Matt 5:43), and hatred toward someone's evil deeds rather than toward the person themselves (Rev 2:6). This includes recognizing who the real "enemy" is (even the possibility that we may be wrong). Before deciding that one person is to blame for everything wrong in our lives, let us ask whether the negative things in our life, or our ill feelings, would be corrected if that person were no longer a problem. The hatred that nailed Jesus to the cross did not go away after his death; let us again overcome evil, even the hatred within us, with good.

June 5

"Take Care How You Hear"

THE SEARCH FOR TRUTH places an obligation both on the sender and on the recipient. To receive truth requires not only an ear that is pointed in the direction of truth (2 Tim 4:4), but a certain mindset conditioning the ears so directed. When receiving any message, one's attitude can affect how they interpret it (for example, a bad mood can cause one to reject the message, regardless of its content). Thus Jesus said, "Take care then how you hear" (Luke 8:18). This includes such things as the fact that it is important that we be careful not only with regard to the truthfulness of the message, but to the proper condition of our heart to receive it. Truth by definition does not change; the human heart, on the other hand, can change with the wind. To take heed to ourselves is necessary for truth to find a proper home, without which the search therefore may have been in vain.

June 6

Will-Worship

WHETHER IT'S CALLING "EVIL good and good evil" (Isa 5:20) or changing what worship is, one of the techniques of the world to satisfy its desires is to redefine truth. Entertainment is basically for our self-satisfaction; worship is unselfish, in that it is an act of reverence or devotion for someone else. When Paul spoke of "will-worship" ("which things have indeed a show of wisdom in will-worship, and humility, and severity to the body; but are not of any value against the indulgence of the flesh," Col 2:23 ASV), his word for "will-worship" is difficult to understand; yet it seems to mean worship that one has contrived themselves, and perhaps is directed toward oneself. Worship is an activity that one directs toward someone other than himself. Will-worship doesn't have to be a literal bowing down to a statue of oneself; it seems it could also be, in today's world, getting dressed, driving to a church building, sitting through and even participating in the worship activities for an hour, but, for example, thinking only of oneself for the entire hour. Since we naturally tend to focus on ourselves anyway, it might become easy to forget what worship is. For this reason it is good to remind ourselves that in worship our thoughts are to be focused on the right object—that is, on God, rather than ourselves. Or, in Jesus' words just before his death, "not my will, but yours, be done" (Luke 22:42).

June 7
"I Am Doing a Work"

WE OFTEN HAVE TROUBLE making sense of our world, especially with regard to the problem of evil, and whether God is doing anything about it. When Habakkuk questioned why evil was seemingly allowed to have free reign in his country (Hab 1:2–4), God assured him that he was doing something about it: "Look at the nations, consider, and be utterly astounded. For I am doing a work in your days (which) you would not believe if told" (Hab 1:5). The reassurance God offers was true for Habakkuk in his time (that is, this verse is not spoken to directly to us today). Yet, Jesus did say that God is at work (John 5:17). When something doesn't make sense to us, such as the problem of evil, this can be an opportunity to develop faith versus concentrating on only solving a problem. The extent to which we see justice in this life must be left up to him; that is, it may seem as if evil is at times allowed to run free. Rather, to trust God based on his word today requires more strength and therefore is better for us. This is in part true because that which is better for us is the development of our spiritual lives, more so than receiving a resolution to our problem (2 Cor 12:9). When problems arise, we can rather focus on the promises of God today, and believe what we are told in his word. Though the message given to Habakkuk was not spoken directly to us, God nevertheless has great things in store for his children (1 Cor 2:9); if we were told what they were we may not believe it anyway.

June 8
The Power of God

THE POWER OF WORDS, and especially Jesus' word, will never go away (Matt 24:35). Human communication has gone from symbols (cuneiform) to words, to symbols (stories in the Middle Ages were usually told in pictures) to words, to words and symbols (emojis in emails). Again, words can be for good or evil; thus, as with many things in the hands of people, the Bible cautions us with regard to their use and possible abuse. James said, "So also the tongue is a small member, yet it boasts of great things. How great a forest is set ablaze by such a small fire!" (Jas 3:5). That against which James cautions us is, however, not the danger of words, but of the abuse of the tongue. Words can be harmful, but only when dispensed by an evil tongue. This is because the tongue reflects that which is in one's heart (Luke 6:45). We control our words by controlling our tongue, and we control our tongue by conditioning our heart. We do this by concentrating on a strong spiritual life, since this includes attention to God's word, the power that conditions our heart (Rom 1:16).

June 9
Always Learning

The Christian has been cleansed in their soul by their obedience to the truth (1 Pet 1:22). Being a Christian includes living a life consistently engaged in learning (the Greek word translated "disciple" has to do with being a learner). Since the pursuit of truth is ongoing (2 Pet 3:18), the pursuit of truth as well as truth itself can both be considered a goal. Without truth, the pursuit of knowledge could be counter-productive, inasmuch as one might thereby be "always learning and never able to arrive at a knowledge of the truth" (2 Tim 3:7).

June 10

"Count Others Better"

HUMILITY IS AN ATTITUDE; being humbled is a condition. The Bible speaks of the importance and of the inevitability of humility; that is, we are again going to be humble (Prov 18:12; Luke 14:11). Being humble is not determined by one's lack of such things as natural talent or money that might distinguish them from others. Rather, in the Bible humility is an attitude one adopts. Thus Paul said, "Do nothing from selfishness or conceit, but in humility count others better than yourselves" (Phil 2:3 RSV). As with many other aspects of the Christian life, this is again the opposite of the natural approach, inasmuch as this is the spiritual approach. The difficulty in adopting this attitude lies partly in the fact that it is unselfish. This verse reflects the attitude of the Christian toward his brethren, that no one in the church is to look down upon another. Rather, being humble means choosing to adopt the mind of Christ (v. 5), which is to be humble, and will ultimately lead to our exaltation.

June 11

Ask for Peace

THE NAME "JERUSALEM" MEANS "city of peace." In Ps 122 the psalmist expresses his joy at being included among his brethren as they go to the house of the Lord (v. 1), which is in Jerusalem (v. 2). He then prays for this his city, which includes a mention of peace and prosperity (vv. 6–8), with the outer frame of the psalm being the house of God (vv. 1, 9). The psalm culminates in v. 9 with the psalmist's desire for good for the house of God: "Let me seek your good for the sake of the house of the LORD our God." For him the house was the tabernacle or temple. We as Christians are told to pray for political good so that we may lead a quiet and tranquil life (1 Tim 2:1–2). We are also told to conduct ourselves properly in the house of God today, which is the church (1 Tim 3:15). To do so will gladden our heart to know that when we go to worship we have gladdened the heart of God.

June 12

"If the Lord Wills"

To contemplate the future can be productive or destructive. Proper planning, such as counting the cost (Luke 14:28) is often essential to success, while worrying about the future is only destructive (both to our physical health as well as to our soul). The Bible therefore warns us against having the wrong kind of attitude in our planning. James taught to be careful when making our plans (Jas 4:13–14), ending with giving us a key to "successful" planning: "instead you ought to say, 'If the Lord wills, we will live and do this or that'" (Jas 4:15). The wise man also stated in Prov 21:31, "The horse is prepared for the day of battle, but deliverance belongs to the Lord." Whether it be for a budget or a battle, the future can be faced with confidence by looking at it spiritually. Planning down to the minutest detail may or may not ensure physical success; the real key to proper planning is spiritual. Otherwise, to build a house without the Lord (Ps 127:1) may cause our labor to be in vain. Proper planning is rather best built upon the statement of Jesus, "not my will, but yours, be done" (Luke 22:42).

June 13

Why Keep Praying?

Jesus' teaching on persistence in prayer in Luke 18 reminds us of the importance of praying regardless of the evident response from God. The parable ends with the king in the parable giving the lady what she asks for ("because this widow keeps bothering me, I will give her justice, so that she will not beat me down by her continual coming," Luke 18:5). But Jesus' teaching is that the listener "ought" always to pray. The Greek word translated "ought" means one is obligated to do it. This suggests that our prayer life should not entirely depend on the response we receive to our prayers; and yet, that we are always to pray. To pray only because we (or in order to) receive a positive response suggests one's heart is harboring a selfish attitude. Though God wants us to have help (Heb 4:16), and perhaps to have what we want, to satisfy selfish desires may not be for our most spiritual good (Jas 4:3). To be persistent in prayer could suggest an unselfish attitude; to stop praying because we didn't receive what we had asked for suggests otherwise. In the parable, however, the lady finally got what she wanted. Persistence in prayer can help us develop spiritually, including overcoming unselfishness, and perhaps receive what we want.

June 14
No More Pain

WE MIGHT SAY THAT pain is a price, and that pleasure carries a price. The price of some immediate pain sometimes carries an eventual reward, such as the pain of exercise bringing good health, or the pain of a financial investment leading to financial gain. Pleasure, however, which is usually immediate, carries a price later. Not that all pleasure is illegitimate; but, as a rule, the more one gives themselves to pleasure, the more pain they are asking for in the future, with the possible ultimate pain of losing their soul (again, this is not to say that all pleasure per se is wrong; but even legitimate pleasures, such as eating, can be abused). Thus Paul said that the younger widow who "giveth herself to pleasure is dead while she lives" (1 Tim 5:6). With the right attitude pain can bring us closer to God (2 Cor 12:10); and pleasure, when treated properly, need not damage our soul. We overcome pain not with pleasure, but with strength that carries us to heaven. There is going to be pain in this life; how we react to pain and how we treat pleasure could determine whether we go to a place with no pain, only pleasure (Rev 21:4).

June 15

Obey from the Heart

DOES GOD ONLY REQUIRE of us accomplishment, activity, or is there another element, something that gives meaning to action? Accomplishing things in this life, such as editing books, are what we as people usually value. To be active can be a good thing, inasmuch as, among other things, activity can speed mental acceptance of an otherwise laborious task. For example, have you ever found yourself involved in something in which you had no initial interest, only to find it becoming enjoyable as you went along? The Bible teaches Christians to be "always abounding in the work of the Lord" (1 Cor 15:58). For our activity to have meaning, however, it must come from the heart. If all God wanted was to see things done, he could have created robots to do the work. The heart is what directs our obedience (Rom 6:17), what leads to obedience (Matt 21:28–31), and what gives action meaning (1 Cor 13:3). Without love, or without the heart, our actions (our accomplishments) may be as a noisy gong or a clanging cymbal (1 Cor 13:1).

June 16

"Jesus Found Him"

JESUS IS LOOKING FOR people to worship him. Surely one of the main reasons for this is that this is what's best for us (God does not need anything we can offer, Ps 50:12). The man in John 9 had been thrown out of his place of worship (the synagogue, John 9:34). After this the Bible states, "Jesus heard that they had cast him out, and having found him he said, 'Do you believe in the Son of Man?'" (John 9:35), after which the man worshiped him (v. 38). God is looking for a certain type of person to worship him (that is, "true worshipers," John 4:23). If we seek we will find (Matt 7:7). If God is looking for us to worship him, including this Sunday, will he find us?

June 17

The Quest for Truth

OUR TAKING DELIGHT IN great accomplishments is sometimes accompanied by a dislike for the process by which we achieve that end result. Truth can be known (John 8:32; 1 John 2:21), it can be done (John 3:21), and it can remain with one (2 John 1:2); yet the search for truth should be an ongoing effort. The Bible's emphasis on growth reminds us of the need to be engaged in a process rather than to complete a task. Peter said, "But grow in the grace and knowledge of our Lord and Savior Jesus Christ" (2 Pet 3:18a). This is also why one can incessantly speak of the concept of truth without it sounding like he has all of the answers. To think of something never getting done might be overwhelming; when looked at spiritually, that is, that the quest for truth is never ending, could provide a perpetual benefit to the soul, inasmuch as to assume such a challenge can provide a consistent means of spiritual growth.

June 18

"The Father Loves Me"

OBEDIENCE CAN BE MANIFESTED in a relinquishing of the will. That is, to obey the wishes of another depends not on how we feel, but on our devotion or desire to please that person. This devotion is included in the quality of love, and can be heard in Jesus' teaching (John 15:14) as well as his example (Acts 10:38). Jesus said, "For this reason the Father loves me, because I lay down my life that I may take it up again" (John 10:17), something he did of his own free will, in response to the commandment he received from his Father (John 10:18 ASV). Jesus' love for his Father was demonstrated in obedience to the Father's commandment. While feelings therefore are surely a part of what governs the human heart, true love can overcome any feelings that might be an obstacle, in order to carry out love's ultimate manifestation, that of bending the will of the heart to the will of another. If the "fruit of the Spirit" (Gal 5:22) is to be manifested in the life of the Christian it will include the quality of love, and therefore will be seen in obedience. "By their fruits ye shall know them" (Matt 7:20 ASV).

June 19

"He That Would Love Life"

PETER, QUOTING Ps 34, gave a prescription for having a good life: "For 'whoever desires to love life and see good days, let him keep his tongue from evil and his lips from speaking deceit; let him turn away from evil and do good; let him seek peace and pursue it'" (1 Pet 3:10–11). Peter is not giving a magic formula for having everything go our way; bad things are going to happen in life. Among the many lessons contained in these poetic verses, two primary points are that these verses have to do with the spiritual qualities of truth and of peace, and that the good things Peter mentions are to be actively sought. Left to itself the tongue is generally an evil thing (Jas 3:6), and man's natural state seems to not be one of peace (Rom 12:18). Almost anything good in life requires effort. When one applies themselves to positive spiritual pursuits, it does not mean they will never have any problems; it does mean they will have "good days," including that all things work together for good (Rom 8:28). Days can be good, viz., one can have a "good" life, when they trust in God, whether their days are pleasant or not.

June 20

"What This Means"

ONE REASON WORDS ARE powerful is because they contain meaning that can affect the soul. Objects can contain meaning, just as one's favorite coffee cup brings them joy when it reminds them of their favorite vacation spot. So there can be more to a word than simply its sound or shape; words can also produce mental images. God's word is powerful because it is truth (John 17:17) and, when acted upon, purifies our soul (1 Pet 1:22). This is not as simple as, for example, only saying the words (Matt 7:21), but rather it is because of the way words affect the soul (for example, to hear such words as "spider" or "Hitler" likely provokes a negative response). Christians should have the ultimate goal of truth, with study as the avenue through which this goal is attained; thus learning is a goal, yet is not an end in itself. To reach truth means not just reading and memorizing words, but striving to uncover the meaning contained in the words. This reality provides both a challenge and an opportunity to the child of God. Jesus rebuked his listeners on one occasion for missing this very point: "And if you had known what this means, 'I desire mercy, and not sacrifice,' you would not have condemned the guiltless" (Matt 12:7).

June 21

"Who Shall Stand?"

THE PSALMIST GAVE A poetic description of the kind of worshiper one should be when presenting themselves in worship to God: "Who will ascend the hill of the LORD? And who will stand in his holy place? The one (with) innocent hands and a pure heart, does not lift his soul to falsehood and has not sworn to deceit" (Ps 24:3–4). The psalmist desired that one bring before God a life characterized by both purity of life and purity of worship. Jesus' blood gives Christians a pure soul (1 John 1:7–9); we bring a pure life to worship. As we approach his throne, it is good to be reminded of the need to have a right relationship with others (Matt 5:23–24), that is neither tarnished by nor causes improper worship (1 Cor 11:17–22). Otherwise our worship may be as unacceptable as described in Amos 5:21, where Israel was told by God, "I hate, I despise your feasts, and I take no delight in your sacred assemblies"; not so much because of the (kind of) worship, but because of the (kind of) worshipers.

June 22

"He Came to Himself"

PERCEPTION CAN GREATLY AFFECT both feelings and understanding. Truth by definition does not change, including what we think of it (see tomorrow's "Daily"). Yet the way we perceive things depends on us, and can affect us differently depending on that perception (Jacob reacted a certain way after being misled by Joseph's brothers regarding the false report of Joseph's death, Gen 37:32–34). This is not meant to put entire responsibility on the recipient; the speaker must speak "truth in love" (Eph 4:15). Yet it can remind us that sometimes having a "change of heart" may depend on the conditions under which a message strikes us. Of both Peter (Acts 12:11) and the prodigal son (Luke 15:17) the Bible states they "came to themselves"; their perception changed. Sin being a state in which man had not been created to live (Gen 2–3), perhaps one needs to "come to himself" or be "pricked in heart" (Acts 2:37) so that he or she can come back to God. Sometimes this requires hearing the gospel message several times, inasmuch as in a different setting the message may affect one differently. When sending (such as the gospel) or receiving a message, it can be good to remember that a rejection is not necessarily forever. Truth does not change, though our heart, and thus our perception, might, a fact concerning which it is good to remember, or, in the words of Jesus, to "take care then how you hear" (Luke 8:18).

June 23

"Your Obedience to the Truth"

THE DEFINITION OF TRUTH is not dependent on our perspective. Neither we nor the church define what truth is (the church is to uphold, rather than define, the truth, 1 Tim 3:15). Some things, such as the kind of music or food one likes, depend on the person. Some things are just true, whether we accept them or not. These include that God's word is truth (John 17:17); God's word is the power to salvation (Rom 1:16), and Jesus' blood removes sin (Eph 1:7). The reason these things are true is because God stated them. Since the truth does not change, what needs to change is one's response to them. By hearing the truth one might change; by acting upon it one changes forever. Peter stated, "Having purified your souls by your obedience to the truth for a sincere brotherly love, love one another earnestly from a pure heart" (1 Pet 1:22). Our perspective doesn't determine right and wrong. Truth does not change; but when truth lands in a good heart (Luke 8:15) it changes the heart for good.

June 24

"In the Heavenly Places"

THE GREEK WORD TRANSLATED "wrestle" appears only in Eph 6:12 in the NT: "for we do not wrestle against flesh and blood, but against the rulers, against the authorities, against the cosmic powers over this present darkness, against the spiritual forces of evil in the heavenly places." Paul doesn't inform, but rather assumes, that Christians are in a struggle. What he does inform his readers of is the kind of struggle in which we are. Being a Christian means that one is assured of such positive life features as peace (Phil 4:7) and security from God (Phil 4:19); yet he or she is nevertheless engaged in a fight. Paul states that our wrestling is against such things as "spiritual forces." We often blame the wrong person, usually the easiest target (perhaps we try to avoid blaming ourselves in order to avoid the truth). If we keep in mind that our struggle as Christians is spiritual, it can help us to abhor evil (Rom 12:9), while loving our enemies (Matt 5:44), and still keep in mind the ultimate field upon which the battle is waged. By concentrating on the spiritual, it can help us to keep in proper focus with whom we ultimately struggle, and thus not put too much emphasis on the physical or temporal. We focus on the spiritual by, among other things, taking up the equipment and the strength God supplies (Eph 6:13–17), and keeping in mind that, as Christians, we will have the ultimate victory where the battle is waged—in heavenly places (Rev 2:10).

June 25
Life Finds a Way

LIKE A BLADE OF grass coming up through a crack in the cement, life always finds a way in spite of the growth of evil. Though we can not know the future, or always know why bad things happen, the Christian has been given the spiritual tools to apply to life and its often negative situations. Whether our problems are solved or not, God has given us the means to avoid letting the past keep us from enjoying the present (Phil 3:13), to overcome a present negative distress (2 Cor 12:10), and to avoid letting the future keep us from getting the most out of the present (Matt 6:34). Outward circumstances can certainly affect us; the more important thing, however, is that the Christian use God's spiritual implements (Eph 6:13–17) to let these seemingly negative things affect us for good. Outward negative circumstances which would otherwise make us weak can make us strong by applying these spiritual tools. No matter what the past has offered, or what the future holds, if we would concentrate on things that are above (Col 3:2) it will help us have a better life here below. Not because of what physically happens, but because of how we approach it spiritually.

June 26

"These Words"

It seems that evil is restless (Prov 4:16; 1 Pet 5:8), while goodness must often be prompted into action. Renewal is necessary to make something new again, but the concept of renewal is something that by definition is going to expire. This is why Christians need to give attention to consistent input of good things (Phil 4:8), Scripture among them being primary. Deuteronomy 6:6–7 reads, "And these words that I command you today are to be on your heart; And you are to inculcate them to your children, and speak of them when you sit in your house, and when you walk in the way, and when you lie down, and when you rise." Whether it be by glancing at a phone or three by five card, or repeating a verse we have memorized, keeping Scripture in our head can help us stay spiritually new and, more importantly, help us avoid the evil that seemingly does not sleep.

June 27

Our Will and God's Will

IT IS NOT WRONG for us to desire and to ask for something from God. Even persistent prayer can be a good thing toward the development of a relationship with God (Luke 18:1–8). When looked at properly, pushing our will in order to get what we want can serve a greater purpose. That is, our desires can be a way of getting to the larger goal of God's will. It seems that God wants us to have what we want within the confines of his will. He thus invites us to express our desires to him (Heb 4:16), and several passages also serve as examples (Jesus in the garden, Matt 26:42; Peter's desire to walk on the water to Jesus was his idea, Matt 14:28; in Acts 21:14, they pressed Paul as far as they could, then said, "The will of the Lord be done"). Rather than asking only to fulfill our selfish desires (Jas 4:3), a larger purpose to our desires, and therefore to our prayers, can be to bring us to the point of leaving everything up to God. Being able to relinquish our will to his may then serve as the ultimate test. It may also serve to help us to get what we want.

June 28

"His Abundant Greatness"

THE PSALMIST CALLED ON God's people to praise God "according to his abundant greatness": "Praise him according to his mighty deeds; praise him according to his abundant greatness" (Ps 150:2). As it were, the psalmist is calling on worshipers to praise God in a way that corresponds to a quality of God, rather than in a way based on ourselves. The Christian is to give in accordance with how he or she has prospered (1 Cor 16:2), is to sing praises when they are cheerful (Jas 5:13), as well as to pray and sing with the spirit and with the understanding (1 Cor 14:15). The psalmist's words suggest, among other things, that our worship is not to be borne of other motivations, such as only out of a desire to receive things from God, or only for the purpose of making us feel better. Rather, this verse can reinforce both the purpose and the level of our worship—that it is to correspond to the abundant greatness of the One who possesses this quality. If it does, our worship will be the best we can offer; that is, it will be offered in faith (Heb 11:4), whether in an abundant amount or not (Mark 12:41–44). Such would surely be pleasing to the One who possesses abundant greatness; and he may bless us accordingly.

June 29

Against the Time to Come

IT IS ALWAYS A good thing, for both practical and spiritual reasons, to be ready. Though we do not know the future, evil has a way of spreading and of being persistent, and it is generally more difficult in life to do the right thing. As Christians we can more likely be victorious in the spiritual battle in which we are engaged if we are ready. The general tone of Paul's passage on the Christian armor (Eph 6:10–18) has to do with being ready, and other passages speak of the need to store up in view of the future (Matt 6:19–20; 1 Tim 6:19). Being prepared can include such things as memorizing Scripture, for example in view of the possibility that the Bible is no longer accessible. Being prepared also means making this effort beforehand, rather than waiting until a moment of distress (in Eph 6:10–20, Paul more than once states, "having done," "having put on," etc.). Bad things are going to happen, especially for the Christian (2 Tim 1:10); if we as Christians are prepared we will more likely win spiritually if not physically. If we are not prepared we could lose in both ways.

June 30
To Be Content

CONTENTMENT COMES FROM WITHIN, rather than from without. Contentment has to do with a conditioning of the heart. Possessions per se are not wrong, though one's life does not consist thereof (Luke 12:15). Possessions and prosperity can also condition the heart in such a way as to destroy contentment. We acquire a state of contentment not through having or not having possessions, but by concentrating on spiritual things (whether we have possessions or not). By learning (including learning how to do without, Phil 4:11), perhaps asking for the minimal (Matt 6:11), and not worrying about tomorrow (Matt 6:34), we can condition our heart to be content. By being content we will be more spiritually fulfilled, because our heart has been conditioned from within rather than from without.

July 1

"Where Is Your Faith?"

JESUS SEEMED SURPRISED, EVIDENTLY disappointed, that the disciples were afraid during the storm in Luke 8. After stilling the storm he said to them, "Where is your faith?" (v. 25), as if he expected them to trust him more (even in a storm). All the disciples apparently wanted was for the storm to stop; their evident fear reflects they didn't trust Jesus. Faith in God includes accepting his promises and (therefore) assuming that he has or will see to our requests (Mark 11:24; Heb 11:1). Adopting this belief is a way of avoiding disappointment in spite of any outcome. Jesus expects us to have adopted this belief. Will he be disappointed to find us being afraid in time of storm (Luke 18:8)? He is expecting us to expect God to have taken care of it.

July 2

"When I Am Afraid"

DIFFERENT LIFE SITUATIONS CAN produce a corresponding mindset, which could then affect our understanding of Scripture. That is, outward circumstances such as persecution can help us learn or apply God's word in a way that we might not have otherwise. The psalmist said, "When I am afraid, as for me, I will trust in you" (Ps 56:3). In Hebrew the word "I" is reflected in this verse three times, one of which is there for emphasis (hence the translation "as for me"). We often have to choose between fear and faith (see, for example, Rev 21:8). Therefore fear, such as of persecution, can be the impetus that causes us to learn God's word. Though we may not welcome that which causes the fear, and we need to overcome fear, the good result of learning God's word can result from distress in life (2 Cor 12:10). We may not be able to control that which produces fear, but we can control whether our heart is destroyed by fear or strengthened by faith through God's word (Rom 10:17).

July 3

"Our Refuge and Strength"

PSALM 46:1 READS: "GOD is our shelter and strength, a very present help in (times of) distress." When we come to him, for example in an avenue of worship, it provides a respite to our soul that we can get in no other way. Whether it be to temporarily escape the growing problem of evil, or simply to gain rest from the ordinary strain of life, to worship in private or with others of a like, precious faith can help the Christian hide for a brief period. Worship also provides strength in many ways, among other things through the knowledge that there are others who believe the same way, especially in a world that does not. The psalmist does not say how he takes refuge in God; that is, it could be by his personal prayers, through the respite of reading God's word (Ps 119:114), or through corporate worship. Yet, like a mother bird caring for her young (Ps 91:1–6; 61:4), taking refuge in God gives him strength to go back to an unfriendly world. Enjoying entertainment, which is basically selfish, can thrill us for a short time, yet can make it more difficult to go back to a perhaps unthrilling life. Worship, by contrast, can give us strength because we can thereby forget our troubles and ourselves for the short time we are engaged therein. God's word gives power (Rom 1:16; Acts 20:32). Running and hiding in life may or may not be a good idea; if we hide away with God on a regular basis, we can gain strength to continue in life.

July 4
Truth Sets Free

TRUTH SETS FREE (JOHN 8:32), and being set spiritually free means going forward. To want to go backward therefore is to reject truth. The Israelites would rather have gone back into slavery than go forward (Num 11:5). Paul told the Galatians that, having been set free, they were not to "submit again to a yoke of slavery" (Gal 5:1). As Americans we have political freedom, and as Christians we have spiritual freedom. In both we should make effort to avoid going backward. As Americans we do so to preserve the political freedom we have had since our founding. As Christians we do so to avoid going back into the slavery of sin (John 8:34). We can do this because we look forward to a better country (Heb 11:16). On we go.

July 5
"I Am Telling You This Now"

WE OFTEN GIVE ADVICE, share information, etc., to help someone solve a problem. Jesus told the disciples what was going to happen to him: "I am telling you this now, before it takes place, that when it does take place you may believe that I am he" (John 13:19). The purpose Jesus gave was so that the disciples would believe in him. Today God's word has been written; that is, he has already given us his word (John 20:30, 31; Jude 3); and the purpose thereof is so that we would believe (whether it be the non-believer's initial acceptance, or the child of God's further growth and spiritual development). Why would God go to the trouble of sending prophet after prophet, many of whom were killed, then his Son, who was killed, then apostles, most of whom were killed, in order to give us his word? God's word may or may not help us fix every situation in life; but God gave us his word so that we would believe. To do so solves a lot of spiritual problems.

July 6

"More Than Conquerors"

PAUL SAID THAT, AS Christians, we are "more than conquerors": "No, in all these things we are more than conquerors through him who loved us" (Rom 8:37). How can one be more than victorious? This is a figure of speech, equivalent to Paul's saying he was "less than the least" (Eph 3:8). The Greek word translated "conqueror" is in a form that means we are victorious now, and the word also has a meaning of being completely victorious (hence many translations have "more than conquerors"). Many things in life (like an on/off switch) either are, or they are not. In the same way in life there are not degrees of victory. Since faithful Christians are assured of winning in the end (Rev 2:10), we therefore can know that such things as tribulation, distress, persecution, etc. (Rom 8:35) do not keep us from the love of Christ, nor should they keep him from our reciprocal love. The seeming defeats of this life, which are physical and therefore temporary, can serve as a reminder that, rather than being defeated, we are spiritually more than conquerors—and that now.

July 7
"Not Destroyed"

"Bad" things are going to happen in life. A loss or setback, as manifested in the physical realm, does not, however, mean total defeat. As noted in yesterday's "Daily," Christians are "more than conquerors" (Rom 8:37). The fact that the Bible tells Christians they win in the end suggests we need to be told in order to be strong and to persist in spite of the bad things that are going to happen. Thus Paul said, "We are afflicted in every way, but not crushed; perplexed, but not driven to despair; persecuted, but not forsaken; struck down, but not destroyed" (2 Cor 4:9). The physical setbacks that befall the Christian need not affect the spiritual health of our soul or our eternal reward to which we look forward. Paul also said, "So we do not lose heart. Though our outer self is wasting away, our inner self is being renewed day by day" (2 Cor 4:16). Satan may think he's winning with physical victories, but he can't touch that which the Christian has been given by God (John 10:29). God can destroy both soul and body in hell (Matt 10:28). Christians may be struck down in life, but we are not destroyed.

July 8
"Thy Will Be Done"

THE IMPORTANCE OF RELINQUISHING our will to God's can be illustrated in many ways. God wants us to submit our requests to him (Heb 4:16); yet he never promised to just give us everything we ask for. Leaving our requests up to God's will is good for our soul, among other things because it is not good for us to receive everything we want (to satisfy a selfish desire usually leaves one wanting more). This tells us that, in order for our will to become more like God's, we must be prepared for some disappointments. Thus Jesus, on the verge of his life coming to an end, requested that he be able to avoid the cross, yet prayed "thy will be done" (Matt 26:39, 42 ASV). To turn our will over to his also demonstrates to God our willingness to relinquish the one thing that causes us to cling selfishly to our desires, rather than allowing him to rule in our heart. We do this by saying (and meaning), "Thy will be done." If God had intended to give us everything for which we ask, we could ask God that we be allowed never to die; even Jesus wasn't granted that request.

July 9
"Worship God"

TWICE IN THE NT appears the phrase "worship God" (Rev 19:10; 22:9). In both places the person being addressed was desiring to worship someone else (the one giving the message). The Greek word translated "worship" in these verses is a command; the second appearance (Rev 22:9) being one of the last commands in the Bible. Though this phrase appears in a specific context, it reminds us of two things: the initial meaning of the phrase serves (indirectly) as an imperative to everyone, that we are to worship God. It also tells us of the apparent truth that we are going to worship something, and that one often must be directed to worship the right thing. We might be inclined to worship something other than God (Matt 15:8–9), whether it be ourselves, the creature rather than the Creator (Rom 1:24–25), or worshiping God incorrectly (John 4:24). Thus we today, as all sometimes fickle humans, need to be told what to do. Do you have plans for Sunday morning?

July 10

"Having Itching Ears"

ONE REASON A DAILY pursuit of truth requires effort is because of the seductiveness of myths. Paul spoke of those who purposely turn from truth to myths: "For the time is coming when people will not endure sound teaching, but having itching ears they will accumulate for themselves teachers to suit their own passions, and will turn away from listening to the truth and wander off into myths" (2 Tim 4:3–4). The ears may be caused to turn from truth to myth because myths can be more appealing, since they scratch the ears. Truth can be difficult (why so many become angry when they have to face it), and Satan offers many seductive promises (2 Cor 11:14). Myths that are intended to deceive amount to lies, since they come from the father of them (John 8:44). What we should look for, therefore, is not necessarily what scratches our ears, but for truth. Truth can be refreshing as well as liberating (John 8:32), yet does require effort and purpose. Both truth and myth lead us somewhere—one leads to freedom, the other to the bondage of sin (John 8:34), and we can't pursue both. To avoid the pain of where myths lead (Rev 21:8), one may need to endure uncomfortableness in favor of truth, which satisfies the soul rather than itching ears.

July 11

"Have This Mind"

PAUL SAID, "HAVE THIS mind in you, which was also in Christ Jesus" (Phil 2:5 ASV). We often like to be able to control things around us, yet it seems we often overlook that we control one of the most powerful sources at our disposal, our mind. Paul's words again tell us that we choose what type of mind we house. In context of Paul's speaking to the church at Philippi as a group (the word translated "you" is plural in Greek), he teaches that the mind we choose should be the same as that of Christ: one characterized by humility (vv. 6–7) and therefore unselfishness, and one of obedience and of service (v. 8). By so choosing, we thereby relinquish control of our will, which could then redound to good things from God to which we may look forward, namely having our humble state reversed (Matt 23:12).

July 12
"Take Wrong"

DOING GOOD AS CHRISTIANS can include not only spreading good, but also making efforts to avoid spreading bad, such as by the way we speak. For example, to raise one's voice in anger, such as at a clerk in a coffee shop, can spread pain. Paul, speaking of something more serious than a clerk getting an order wrong, said, "Why not rather take wrong?" (1 Cor 6:7). In such situations the Christian has a choice of whether to react negatively, and thus to continue spreading pain, or to offer a gentle answer and thus turn away the anger (Prov 15:1). Arguments basically die with agreement. By keeping and applying a spiritual mindset, even such things as a simple transaction gone wrong can be an opportunity, however small, to glorify God. Not that feelings are the most important thing; but the heart can be a conduit for the reception of truth (Eph 4:15). "Be not overcome with evil, but overcome evil with good" (Rom 12:21). Even if it means getting the wrong kind of coffee.

July 13
God's Word Unites

UNITY AMONG PEOPLE IS always a pleasant thing (Ps 133:1), inasmuch as God hates division (Prov 6:16–19). Naomi, whose name means "pleasantness" was harmoniously united with Ruth (Ruth 1:16–17). Unity can be forged on the basis of many things; among God's people the common denominator that should bind them together is his word. Jesus prayed for those who accept the apostles' word (John 17:20), "that they also may be in us, so that the world may believe that you have sent me" (John 17:21). Division can exist within a country, a family, or oneself (Jas 1:6–8), the latter of which James said is due to doubt, or a lack of faith, which amounts to a lack of God's word (Rom 10:17). To bring harmony to a nation, a family, or one's soul, a unity bound together by truth is that which pleases God; it is a pleasant thing.

July 14
Pierced or Cut?

HEARING THE TRUTH IS going to affect the heart. While the response is unpredictable, perhaps even by the person themselves, the truth is powerful enough to provoke the heart (hence the gospel's being called the "power of God," Rom 1:16, and the "sword of the Spirit," Eph 6:17). Two of these possible responses include being "pierced through the heart" (Acts 2:37, author's translation) and "cut to the heart" (Acts 5:33 ASV; these are two different expressions in the original Greek). Each of these phrases is a metaphoric description of how the truth affected the listeners, the first positive, the second negative. These expressions reflect both the power of the sword of the Spirit, as well as the unpredictability of the human heart. Truth, by definition, does not change; the human heart can. The effect of this sword in both examples was pain; but the pain of the unchanging truth can be pleasurable, especially knowing that it can affect the heart so that it changes the soul for all eternity. In a way, whether our heart is pierced or cut is up to us. Certainly what we do with the truth afterward is.

July 15

"The Renewal of Your Mind"

OUR MIND, LIKE ANY storage space, needs to be renewed from time to time. This physical need is fulfilled through sleep; yet there is also a need to spiritually renew because of the thoughts that fill our head. Since sleep is a natural process, physical renewal acquired thereby requires our attention. Paul spoke of the renewing of our mind in Rom 12:2: "do not be conformed to this world, but be transformed by the renewal of your mind, that by testing you may discern what is the will of God, what is good and acceptable and perfect." Renewal is here set in contrast to being conformed to the world. The Greek word translated "be conformed" contains an image of being squeezed into a mold. By living the Christian life, including setting our eyes on heaven (Col 3:2), filling our head with the word (Deut 6:6–9), and spending time in prayer (Eph 6:18; 1 Thess 5:17), we can renew our mind, and thereby avoid being conformed to the world. Rather than be forced into the mold of a world characterized by death and decay, the Christian enjoys a new life from the time it begins (Rom 6:4; 2 Cor 5:17) until we transition from this world to a place where the newness never ends (Rev 21:4). In the meantime, we renew our mind in view thereof.

July 16
Each One Win One

WHILE EVANGELISM IS A duty of all Christians (Matt 28:18–21), it seems proper to raise the question of what the goal of evangelism should be. That is, should we purpose to baptize all seven billion people in the world ourselves, to baptize just one, or something in between? Should we put a number on our efforts (the book of Acts consistently takes account of the numerical size of the church)? Such questions may serve to illustrate that evangelism, as with other aspects of the Christian life, can be looked at spiritually. That is, evangelism can again be looked at as something we are to be engaged in as well as something to get done. Everyone in the world needs to be right with God. We can also, however, emphasize the spiritual aspects of evangelism, that is, of having and aiming toward a goal, or being evangelistic versus merely completing a job. To do so can possibly contribute to our spiritual growth, as well as to fulfill this important duty, and hopefully save just one soul for eternity. Having a goal helps us spiritually by helping us to become, rather than only to be, active.

July 17

Abide Where You Are Planted

PRODUCING FRUIT IS NOT a reward for being a fruit tree, but rather the natural result of the tree's growing to maturity. One reason trees bear fruit is because they don't move. Trees are planted, rather than plant themselves (Ps 1:3). In Ps 1, the child of God is compared to a tree which is planted, and thus has a stability which fosters fruit-bearing. In like manner, the Christian today is told to "abide" in Jesus so that he or she can produce fruit: "Abide in me, and I in you. As the branch cannot bear fruit by itself, unless it abides in the vine, neither can you, unless you abide in me" (John 15:4). Like a tree Christians are planted, in that they are added to the church (Acts 2:47), and transferred into the kingdom (Col 1:13). They are then to abide in Christ, in that they are to stay with the teaching through which they became Christians (Col 2:6–7). God has done his part is putting us where we are; we are to do ours in staying there (Col 2:12). In this way we can mature in Christ as a mature fruit-bearing tree.

July 18

A Bunch of Rubbish

THE REASON A CAT can scratch a piece of expensive furniture and it be upsetting to the owner, while the cat couldn't care less, is because of the way we count the furniture. Paul's attitude toward his accomplishments and status in life was that he considered everything a bunch of rubbish when compared with Christ: "Indeed, I count everything as loss because of the surpassing worth of knowing Christ Jesus my Lord. For his sake I have suffered the loss of all things and count them as rubbish, in order that I may gain Christ" (Phil 3:8). The word "count" here has to do with the value Paul places on these things (not whether these things are valuable). The word "rubbish" means any kind of refuse (such as garbage). Both of these are used in comparison with the knowledge of Christ. The things we have, accomplish, etc., are going to go away. The word of Christ saves (1 Pet 1:22), and is not going away (Matt 24:35). The way we count the things of this life can be a reflection of the way we count the knowledge of Christ, which determines our eternal state.

July 19
"Be Steadfast"

As Christians we have a need both to hang in there, as well as to press on, in life. Evil is a restless and growing force, that is pervasive regardless of what we think about it. If we do nothing, evil will likely find us (1 Pet 5:8). The Christian has a need both to be active as well as to be strong (Rom 12:21; Eph 6:10). Paul thus said: "Therefore, my beloved brothers, be steadfast, immovable, always abounding in the work of the Lord, knowing that in the Lord your labor is not in vain" (1 Cor 15:58). The first two words Paul uses ("steadfast, immovable") have to do with not giving up, among other things, so that we can be strong against evil. We have to press on no matter how difficult life is. The harvest fields are white for an evangelistic harvest (John 4:35). Whether it be in this specific area, or in life in general, the one thing we can't do is quit. We can be about the work of the Lord by being steadfast and unmovable. Moving forward is accomplished in part by holding our ground.

July 20
"Them That Call 'Evil' 'Good'"

THE WORLD LOVES TO redefine things, and to name things according to their opposite. While the effects of so doing are many, one is that such action blurs an understanding of truth in the specific realm to which this applies. For example, to call "evil" "good" and "good" "evil" (Isa 5:20) thereby blurs a clear definition of both. Since these concepts are defined in the Bible, it means that God has defined them, thus man is not at liberty to attempt to redefine them. Truth will never go away, and truth sometimes shines through to blind people's misperceptions. Such is a reminder not only of the existence of truth, but of its eternal nature, both to break through and shatter people's belief in myths, as well as to affect the soul, so that it also endures for all of eternity. We purify our soul "by your obedience to the truth" (1 Pet 1:22). One can't change truth, even by giving it another label; but truth can change the soul and make it something new (2 Cor 5:17).

July 21

A Joyful Shout

THE PSALMIST DIRECTED, "SHOUT joyfully to the LORD" (Ps 100:1). When we sing to God, can there be different qualities to this expression? Singing can be a reflection of what is in the soul. Worship can be offered with different manifestations of the heart, including such things as being a cheerful giver (2 Cor 9:7) and singing and praying with understanding (1 Cor 14:15). A joyful shout is offered out of joy (one of the qualities of the fruit of the Spirit, Gal 5:22), and thus to offer a joyful shout can bring joy to the singer as well as the hearer. The Hebrew word translated "shout joyfully" in Ps 100:1 appears in other contexts regarding battle, including as a shout of victory (Judg 7:21). As Christians we win, both now (1 Cor 15:57), and in the future (Rev 2:10b, conditioned upon our faithfulness). Knowing this, as well as the joy that is part of the Christian life, can help us offer joyful worship to God, and hopefully thereby give him joy.

July 22

"His Kingdom and His Righteousness"

CERTAINLY FULFILLING JESUS' WORDS in Matt 6:33 has to do with carrying the action he commands ("seek") as well as the importance he places on the action ("first"). He said: "But seek ye first his kingdom, and his righteousness; and all these things shall be added unto you" (Matt 6:33 ASV). Both of these, however, are given their fullest meaning by the objects to which they apply: "his kingdom and his righteousness." That is, one might seek, and concentrate on putting something first, perhaps without even being aware of what it is. Unless we are aware of what we seek, both the action and the priority we place thereupon may be misguided. That is, it is possible that we are deluding ourselves into thinking we are putting God first when we are actually putting ourselves first. It seems important, therefore, to emphasize that the two things Jesus says to seek first have to do, not with ourselves, but with God. Fulfilling the teaching of Matt 6:33 begins with undoing our will in favor of God's will; that is, we are to seek "his kingdom and his righteousness." This is a means of turning our will over to God's, as Jesus in the garden (Luke 22:42), and is a key to receiving the things God promises to add to us.

July 23

See and Know, Consider and Ponder

God stated in Isa 41 that he would provide for and not forsake the poor, "so that they would see and know, and would consider and ponder together, that the hand of the Lord has done this, and the Holy One of Israel has created it" (Isa 41:20). Becoming right with God begins in the mind (Rom 10:17); maturity in Christ involves arriving at the meaning of Scripture (Heb 5:14). The four words "see," "know," "consider," and "understand" suggest both emphasis and progression. To understand Scripture it is necessary not just to repeat the words, but to arrive at the meaning thereof; there is a progression of learning that ends with understanding, inasmuch as therein is found the will of God (1 Cor 2:10). To not do so suggests one has halted on the path of learning set forth in Isa 41, and may mean one is like the "ignorant and unstable" who wrestle with things hard to understand, to their own destruction (2 Pet 3:16).

July 24

"Perplexed, but Not to Despair"

WHILE IT IS ESSENTIAL for Christians to understand Scripture (see yesterday's "Daily"), it is not necessarily essential for us to understand life. That is, we may not always understand why life is the way it is, whether our circumstances be positive or negative. Paul said he and his coworkers were "perplexed, but not driven to despair" (2 Cor 4:8). Paul's response to otherwise crushing circumstances was to be determined that they would not drive him to despair. There is enough negative in life that it would be easy for anyone to despair (the word has to do with giving up, even to the point of giving up on life, 2 Cor 1:8). The means by which Paul avoided this despair was spiritual, and based on the word of God. In the same context he described their work in the gospel, saying, "Since we have the same spirit of faith according to what has been written, 'I believed, and so I spoke,' we also believe, and so we also speak" (v. 13). Sometimes the only way to make sense of life is by reasoning, not to determine why life is the way it is, but to find reason through Scripture.

July 25
Being Jesus' Friend

IN JOHN 13 JESUS told the disciples with regard to his coming betrayal, "I am telling you this now, before it takes place, that when it does take place you may believe that I am he" (v. 19). Jesus gave them this information, that is, his word, for the purpose of getting them to believe. A few chapters later in John he said, "If you love me, you will keep my commandments (John 14:15), and "you are my friends if you do what I command you" (John 15:14). The common thread that connects belief with love and with Jesus' friendship is acceptance of and obedience to his word. After being told his word, we know; upon accepting his word we believe. Belief, and therefore love, find their ultimate expression in obedience (John 13:19), and through this we become Jesus' friend.

July 26

Exalt and Bow

IN HIS CALL TO worship, the psalmist in Ps 99 uses two particular words that remind us of the proper perspective in worship. He begins with a third word, "praise," in v. 3. Then in vv. 5 and 9, which read almost identically, appear the two words "exalt" and "worship." Verse 5 reads, "Exalt the LORD our God; worship at his footstool! Holy is he!" The Hebrew word translated "exalt" literally means "to lift"; the word translated "worship" literally means "to bow." These two words, which in effect are contrasting, remind us again that worship is for the primary purpose of praising God, rather than for our satisfaction. It is, however, an irony in life that selfless actions are basically good for us. In both verses the call to worship is based on the fact that God is holy, with v. 9 being more climactic ("because God is holy"). Though Christians are also to be holy, including before entering his presence (1 Cor 11:29), by lifting his name, combined with our own humility (Luke 18:9–14), we thereby contribute to our holiness and to a stronger relationship with God. In the words of the apostle John, "He must increase, but I must decrease" (John 3:30).

July 27

Happiness from Without; Joy Within

HAPPINESS IS THE RESULT of things that happen to us (see "hap" in such words as *perhaps* and *haphazard*). Thus such things as good weather, a good meal, and good relations make us happy. The absence (or if they be more in the negative) of these things might make us unhappy. Joy, on the other hand, is a spiritual quality, that does not depend on outward circumstances. Joy is the result of a spiritual life, that is, the "fruit of the Spirit." Thus, from Gal 5:22 the Christian can see that by concentrating on a spiritual life, they can be joyful whether or not the weather is good, they have good food to eat, etc. Galatians 5:22–23 reads, "But the fruit of the Spirit is love, joy, peace, patience, kindness, goodness, faithfulness, gentleness, self-control; against such things there is no law." While happiness can possibly be controlled by attention to physical things, joy is the result of our attention to spiritual things. By concentrating on such things as prayer and continued knowledge of God's word we can, like Jesus, endure negative physical things in view of joy (Heb 12:2; Jas 1:2). Temporal happiness depends on what is without; eternal joy rests within.

July 28

"The God to Whom I Belong"

To be owned by no one is to be a slave. That is, total freedom is only true insofar as one is bound by constraints. As Christians we have been redeemed, or bought, and therefore we belong to someone else; we have been set free (Gal 3:1) to be indentured (1 Pet 2:16). It is not beneficial in life to have no restraints whatsoever; a train off of its tracks is "free," but can't go anywhere. So as Christians we are indentured by the fact that we belong to God. Belonging to God means that our freedom is limited by such things as our need to bring glory to him (1 Cor 6:20), but also that God is watching over us for our good. Both of these ideas are embedded in Paul's admonition in Acts 27:23: "for this very night there stood before me an angel of the God to whom I belong and whom I worship." God cares for us in part because he paid such a high price (that is, his Son; John 17:9) to make us his possession. Satan paid no price, so we only belong to him to the extent to which we render voluntary service to him (John 8:34). We are going to serve someone (Rom 6:16). We must therefore choose to obey the One who paid the price, and who therefore owns us. Like a train confined to its tracks, serving the One who owns us is the only way to be free.

July 29
When I Am Afraid

It has been said that, for most people, 80 percent of life is ordinary, day-to-day, and 20 percent consists of out-of-ordinary circumstances or events. Critical moments in life can be the best occasion to reinforce Scripture, inasmuch as this is often when the soul is more strongly affected. Thus we might recall Scripture when tempted (Matt 4:7), when undergoing tragedy (Matt 27:46), or when simply afraid. The psalmist again said, "In God—I will praise his word—in God I have put my trust. I will not fear. What can flesh do to me?" (Ps 56:3–4). God directed his nation of old to dwell on Scripture at all times (Deut 6:6–9); for Christians today, this might be "in season and out of season" (2 Tim 4:2; Eph 5:15–17). Perhaps a good reason for maintaining a focus on Scripture at all times is so that when the 20 percent happens it will be easier to recall it, not so much to solve our problems, but to impact our soul.

July 30

Picking Up the Leftovers

AFTER JESUS HAD FED the five thousand (John 6:1–14) he directed the disciples to pick up what was left over (v. 12; the miracle is recorded in all four Gospels, but only John tells us that Jesus so instructed the disciples). Though we're not told why, there may be other reasons besides the obvious one of making sure they had enough food for the future (they were, after all, well fed after having almost no food at all). Picking up the leftovers could suggest the spiritual importance one places on food. Perhaps this is one reason we see Jesus giving thanks before eating (John 6:11). To show appreciation for help received when there is no longer a serious need could reflect a more sincere heart. Like the spiritual food of Scripture we recall during times such as tragedy (see yesterday's "Daily"), the obtaining and eating of food, especially when the need is great, can be looked at as a moment not only when life is sustained, but also when the soul can be greatly affected. A spiritual attitude toward food can be demonstrated by asking for today's food (Matt 6:11, "give us this day our daily bread"), and being content with the food we have (1 Tim 6:8) The way we treat the physical (such as our bodies, 1 Cor 6:19–20) may be a reflection of the importance we place on the spiritual, including such things as our appreciation toward the One who gave it.

July 31
"Lifting Up Holy Hands"

WHEN PAUL DIRECTED IN 1 Tim 2:8, "I desire then that in every place the men should pray," he continued with the instruction, saying "lifting holy hands without anger or quarreling" (1 Tim 2:8). It seems that the Scripture teaching in this verse is that the worshiper is to bring a certain kind of life, manifested by "holy hands," rather than making sure they physically lift their hands. Lifting the hands is not as important as the kind of hands we lift (several psalms, such as 134, speak of lifting hands in worship). The NT speaks of having a certain posture in worship, though the worship is unacceptable because of the heart behind it. Thus Jesus said many honor him with their lips, "but their heart is far from me" (Matt 15:8 ASV). It is the life we bring to God, as well as our engaging in the proper avenues, that makes our worship acceptable or unacceptable. As it were, the important thing is then the effect our worship has on God, rather than the other way around. Our holy life pleases God through the designated avenues of worship, rather than worship (including in altered forms) pleasing us.

August 1
I Can through Him

Paul's declaration that "I can do all things through him who strengthens me" (Phil 4:13) may sound as if Paul is declaring he can do anything and everything that comes to his mind. The fact that we are bound by the natural limitations of the physical world (2 Cor 4:16), combined with logic, suggests another meaning (for example, it would be impossible for one to get a running start and jump to the moon). The phrase translated "through him" is literally in Greek "in him," which suggests Paul's meaning is to be understood with regard to the spiritual realm (or governed by spiritual things). With power derived from the word (Eph 3:16) our spirit can be empowered to overcome physically difficult or even seemingly impossible situations. In context Paul is speaking of financial circumstances (vv. 11–12). Our limitations suggest that Paul is alluding to other aspects within our control, such as working harder, etc., as well as to spiritual strength to possibly overcome physical circumstances. With faith as a mustard seed (Matt 17:20) we may not be able to jump to the moon, but in Christ we have a strength to remove, or even to leap over, any "mountain" that may be in our way.

August 2
"Every Need"

THE PHRASE TRANSLATED "EVERY need" in Phil 4:19 is one word in Greek, and is a form of the same word "all things" in v. 13 (see yesterday's "Daily"). Verse 19 reads: "And my God will supply every need of yours according to his riches in glory in Christ Jesus" (Phil 4:19). Knowing that there may be times in life when we seem to not have what we physically need suggests that during those times God is perhaps meeting another, that is, a spiritual need. Such a possibility reminds us both that God's got this, and that, to make sense of life, we must often look at it spiritually. God gives us the ability to face life and to overcome it, whether the physical situation meets our preconceived expectations or not. Paul in this verse also uses the word "in," which is the same in Greek as the word "through" in v. 13. In Christ and through Christ one has not only ability, but also has the meeting of their needs, whether or not it matches what we think. Like a child telling their parent they "need" a cookie when the parent knows better, God knows what we need. The answer is spiritual.

August 3
"That It May Rest upon Me"

Paul said that he boasted in his weaknesses, "so that the power of Christ may rest" upon him. Second Corinthians 12:9 reads, "'My grace is sufficient for you, for my power is made perfect in weakness.' Therefore I will boast all the more gladly of my weaknesses, so that the power of Christ may rest upon me." The Greek word translated "rest" here suggests permanence. It is related to the Greek word translated "dwelt" in John 1:14, which states that the word became flesh and "dwelt" among us. Both have a meaning of "pitch a tent." The form used by Paul is, however, stronger than John 1:14, and appears only in this verse. Jesus said that his stay on earth was temporary, yet he promised to provide a means of power after his departure (that is, the Holy Spirit for the apostles, Mark 9:1; John 16:13; the word as well for us today, Heb 4:12). The power of God can be a source of abiding strength to help Christians during difficult times. Times of trouble that bring weakness are not permanent; God's power is (Matt 24:35; 1 Pet 1:23).

August 4
What Did You Expect?

HAVING AN ATTITUDE OF expectation can foster faith in God. To unexpectedly receive something good can naturally bring delight. An expectation born of arrogance, or without God, likely does not bring delight; the arrogant may not be surprised when their desires are fulfilled because it is they who accomplished it (see perhaps Jas 4:13–15). The psalmist said, "And take pleasure in the LORD, so that he would give you your heartfelt requests" (Ps 37:4). Jesus said the Christian can expect God to take care of their requests (Mark 11:24). Not that we are guaranteed to receive whatever we ask for (1 John 5:14), but that we can use expectation to govern our heart for the purpose of conditioning faith. The arrogant assume things are going to go their way because of who they are. The faithful assume that things are going to go God's way. Such an attitude fosters faith and can bring delight upon their fulfillment since we know not the outcome beforehand. We can expect the best when we leave everything up to God, because what's best is God's will; and therein the child of God delights.

August 5

"While I Have My Being"

MAN WAS DESIGNED TO praise, and God is to be praised. In Ps 146, the psalmist recognized that his life, as long as it lasted, was for praising God: "Let me praise the LORD during my life; let me sing praises to my God while I am still going" (Ps 146:2). God is to be praised as creator of the physical world (v. 6), as the one who oversees the spiritual concepts of truth and justice (vv. 6–7), and as one who cares for the needy (vv. 7–9). Unlike human rulers (v. 3), God will reign forever (v. 10); and this gives the worshiper a hope that transcends any person or promise in life (v. 5). We praise God because only he will always be there. If we do, as part of a right relationship with him, we will be there after our being on earth ends as well (Rev 14:7); for this we were designed.

August 6

"One That Is of the Truth"

JESUS SAID, "EVERY ONE that is of the truth heareth my voice" (John 18:37 ASV). To be "of the truth" is to be identified as one given to truth (just like those "of faith" in Gal 3:7). Truth can be challenging for everyone; yet one can adopt a heart that is inclined toward truth, and therefore belong to this class (perhaps similar to one's being "of America"). To "hear the voice of" in biblical Hebrew means "to obey." Is Jesus saying one who is given to truth will be obedient, that one can know that they are of truth because they are obedient (Matt 7:20), or both? While there may be many facets to Jesus' statement, the logic includes such things as Jesus himself is truth (John 14:6), and that truth requires obedience (1 Pet 1:22). To be "of truth" is to be one that loves Jesus (John 14:15), something one can know by their obedient life.

August 7
"According To"

Two things that are to reside in the heart of the Christian are God's will and God's power. With these two things both the Christian and his God can do wonderful things. Paul said, "Whereunto I labor also, striving according to his working, which worketh in me mightily" (Col 1:29 ASV). Paul worked according to the working of God (Paul also spoke of God working his will in the life of the Christian in Phil 2:13). God can do amazing things in the life of the Christian according to the power residing in the Christian. Paul also said, "Now to him who is able to do far more abundantly than all that we ask or think, according to the power at work within us" (Eph 3:20). The gospel, or God's word, is spoken of as "the power" in Rom 1:16. The basis for the Christian doing good work for God, and for God doing wonderful things for the Christian, is according to that which is in the heart of the Christian.

August 8
"I Am Not Alone"

IN JOHN 16:32 JESUS said the disciples would leave him alone, "and yet I am not alone, because the Father is with me" (ASV). How can one be alone, yet not alone? As often in Jesus' speech, he is adding another dimension to the realm of which he is speaking; in this case, that the Father, who is Spirit (John 4:24) is with him. All too often we speak in terms limited in dimension. Naturally the primary way we look at life is natural; we think of "bread" as something to eat, of "water" as something to drink, and of money as something to spend (or something we owe). These words can however be used to speak not only of the natural, but of the spiritual (such as Jesus did in John 4:32–34). In John 16:32 Jesus is speaking of being alone physically versus spiritually. The Christian today can know that God gives us spiritual bread (John 6:33–35) and living water (John 4:10–14), and that Jesus is always with us (Matt 28:18–20). Inasmuch as Christians live by the Spirit (Gal 5:25), we are therefore, like Jesus, not alone; even though we may be alone.

August 9
"The Lord Has Taken Away"

Pivotal moments in life, such as times of loss, can prove whether we have or are able to have a proper attitude. Thus, when we suffer serious loss, we can adopt one of several attitudes, including anger over having lost it; fear over the prospect of replacing it (such as with regard to financial loss); or gratitude for having been given it in the first place. In the first round of losses Job lost just about everything. His answer was "naked I came out of my mother's womb, and naked I will return there. The Lord has given, and the Lord has taken; may the name of the Lord be blessed" (Job 1:21). Job's answer reflects several important thoughts, including that he recognized that God is ultimately responsible for what Job had, thus Job therefore praises God for it; that whether Job kept what he had is up to God; and, instead of focusing on the physical things he lost, Job instead chose to focus on the spiritual element of God's will. Good things, such as an incredible answer to prayer, can evoke one kind of attitude or emotion; when we've lost it all can be both a proving ground for what is in our heart, as well as an opportunity to focus on the spiritual—like Job.

August 10
"A Mantle of Praise"

WORSHIPING GOD AGAIN CAN benefit the worshiper because proper worship is fundamentally unselfish. Thus God through Isaiah states that he would give the recipients "a cloak of praise instead of a faint spirit; that they may be called terebinths of righteousness, the planting of the LORD, to adorn himself" (Isa 61:3). Through worship one can come before God and have his garments changed from a "faint spirit" to a "cloak of praise." Among other things, God here promised the hearers stable conditions (v. 4), which allowed them to be able to worship God. Jesus applied vv. 1 and 2 to himself in Luke 4:18–19. While lifting our voice in praise can lift our spirits, the ultimate purpose of worship is "that he may be glorified." By clothing oneself in Christ (Gal 3:27) and assuming a "cloak of praise" it can change a "faint spirit," making one a "terebinth of righteousness." That is, worship can benefit the worshiper, because it glorifies the One worshiped.

August 11
Patience of Hope

HOPE IS A POWERFUL force because it means both that we have something to hope in, and that we don't have the thing for which we hope. Paul said: "For in this hope we were saved. Now hope that is seen is not hope. For who hopes for what he sees?" (Rom 8:24). While it is good to have our needs and desires fulfilled, unfulfilled needs and desires can give us something to look forward to, and therefore can serve as a motivator to keep going in life; it is good to have the goal of having a goal (1 Thess 1:3). A life with God means one has hope (Eph 2:12), which can elevate our outlook above even the reality of death (1 Thess 4:13). While at times in life it seems we have to "hope against hope" (Rom 4:18), with God we can overcome negative thoughts that may accompany unfulfilled needs. One day our hope as Christians will be realized. In the meantime having hope gives us something to look forward to because of Christ, Who is our hope (1 Tim 1:1).

August 12

Strength to Carry On

WHILE STRENGTH IS NECESSARY to get through this life, our failing physical strength is a reminder that our physical life will come to an end. Another kind of strength is available to sustain us until that time. God's word provides a strength we can't acquire anywhere else. As Paul was preparing to separate from the elders of Ephesus his parting words were "and now I commend you to God and to the word of his grace, which is able to build you up and to give you the inheritance among all those who are sanctified" (Acts 20:32). Paul's admonition includes entrusting the elders to God's word which, Paul said, "is able to build you up." God's word is the power that can give us strength if we avail ourselves of it, and through which God can work in our lives (Eph 3:20). To make use of it can give us an increasing spiritual strength while we endure a decreasing physical strength (2 Cor 4:16). It is also a strength we owe to God in return (that is, to love him with all the strength, Mark 12:33). With God's word building us up, we can not only continue to run the race (1 Cor 9:24), but even become stronger as we do so. As we increase his word we increase in strength and in love for God.

August 13
"Conformed to the Image of His Son"

PAUL SPOKE OF THE Christian's being conformed to the image of Christ: "for those whom he foreknew he also predestined to be conformed to the image of his Son, in order that he might be the firstborn among many brothers" (Rom 8:29). Being conformed is different from conforming oneself. The world would love to, is trying to, and in many ways is succeeding in shaping people according to its mold. Evil is not content to just let good people be (Isa 59:15). We have a choice whether to let the world squeeze us into its mold or to become molded according to the image of Christ. Through such things as the renewing of our mind (Rom 12:2) and avoiding former sinful passions (1 Pet 1:14) that is, through maintaining a strong spiritual life, we can be properly molded. If we do nothing the world will likely form us into its mold. We are going to be conformed to something; if our soul is conformed to the image of Christ, the result of this creation could be the pronouncement of God, that it is "very good" (Gen 1:31).

August 14
The Mind's Eye

AN OPHTHALMOLOGIST TOLD ME that what is good for the heart is good for the eyes. This is of course regarding the physical heart. A healthy spiritual heart can also affect our spiritual eyes. Jesus said, "The eye is the lamp of the body. So, if your eye is healthy, your whole body will be full of light, but if your eye is bad, your whole body will be full of darkness. If then the light in you is darkness, how great is the darkness" (Matt 6:22–23). The heart is the seat of the emotions and is conditioned by the use of the mind. Thus we believe in our heart (Rom 10:10) after hearing (with the mind, Rom 10:17); we obey from the heart (Rom 6:17), and we can become hardened due to disbelief or improper understanding (Eph 4:18). If we give diligence to have a healthy spiritual heart our soul, as represented by the spiritual eyes, will also be healthy. Thus we strive to "keep our heart" (Prov 4:23) and to have a pure heart (Ps 51:10) by diligent attention to a proper spiritual life, and thereby have healthy spiritual eyes. If we set the eye of our mind on things that are above (Col 3:2) one day we will, with our spiritual eyes, see the King (Rev 22:4) whom we obeyed from the heart.

August 15
Preparing for Worship

WHILE SPONTANEOUS EVENTS SUCH as entertainment can thrill the soul, other things are seemingly made better by being prepared for them. It seems that this is especially true when that in which we are engaged requires something of us (such as education or work). While the NT speaks of a "day of preparation" as observed by the Jews, this teaching was evidently not continued by Christians. Yet the NT does speak of planning our giving (1 Cor 16:2; 2 Cor 9:7), of singing a certain type of song in worship (Eph 5:19), and of offering certain kinds of prayers (1 Tim 2:1–8). The sermon (Matt 15:7) could be enhanced for the listener by a prior familiarity with the text being shared. All of these suggest a benefit to preparing for worship beforehand. Such things as preparing our clothes and scraping the ice off the car in preparation for worship are important; being spiritually prepared could make worship more meaningful for us and, seemingly more importantly, draw us closer to God. God has a place prepared both for his people (John 14:2) and for those not in a right relationship with him (Matt 25:41). Being prepared for worship could draw us closer to him, as we look forward to what God has prepared for those who love him (1 Cor 2:9).

August 16
A Need for Faith

LIKE THE DISCIPLES (LUKE 17:5), we should want to increase our faith. One thing we can do in this regard is to positively concentrate on, and even take pleasure in, our unfulfilled needs. In many ways it can be spiritually better to have something to look forward to rather than to have it. This seems to be why Paul said he took pleasure in, among other things, "necessities": "wherefore I take pleasure in weaknesses, in injuries, in necessities, in persecutions, in distresses, for Christ's sake: for when I am weak, then am I strong" (2 Cor 12:10 ASV). For Paul the goal here was not necessarily to have his physical necessities resolved, but was rather spiritual, "so that the power of Christ may rest upon me." Naturally it is good to have needs met (Phil 4:16). Yet the perhaps physical pain of having to bear an unfulfilled need can be an opportunity to grow in spiritual strength, that is, to increase our faith. Rather than concentrating on the pain of the need, Paul chose to concentrate on the pleasure of what it meant; that is, that this physical weakness would mean spiritual strength through God's power. Receiving what we need in life is good; not having our needs fulfilled could be better, in that this could be the opportunity to increase our otherwise lacking faith.

August 17

"Always to Pray"

IN ADDITION TO CONCENTRATING positively on an unfulfilled need (see yesterday's "Daily"), the Christian can further instill faith by acting thereupon through persistently asking God for help with the need. In the parable in Luke 18 Jesus spoke of a lady who kept coming to the judge for help with her adversary. The judge's answer in seeming frustration was "yet because this widow keeps bothering me, I will give her justice, so that she will not beat me down by her continual coming" (v. 5). While the lessons in this passage are many, Jesus among other things teaches that one ought "always to pray" (v. 1). Such persistence can be faith-building as well as a reflection of belief that God is a rewarder of those who seek him (Heb 11:6). To use an unfulfilled need to seek God's grace in time of need (Heb 4:16) could mean the Son of Man will not be disappointed when he returns to seek faith on the earth (Luke 18:8). Persistence in prayer is one of the keys to having our needs fulfilled and, perhaps more importantly, to demonstrating to God that we believe him.

August 18
Giving Life to Faith

IN ADDITION TO A positive attitude (see the day before yesterday's "Daily") and persistent prayer (see yesterday's "Daily"), faith can also grow in the life of the Christian by one's applying action to their faith. While God is the giver of life (1 Tim 6:13), we can give life to faith by combining it with works. James said, "For as the body apart from the spirit is dead, so also faith apart from works is dead" (Jas 2:26). To put belief into action by doing our part to satisfy the need is to give life to our faith, and only by having life can our faith grow. Mental exercises such as prayer are essential but, based on James' words, these may be said to be foundational aspects (such as planting and tending a seed) which yet do not give life to faith. If we only take action for the purpose of fixing problems, such action may work to prevent faith from producing life; if we act for spiritual reasons, we could bring life to an otherwise dead entity. Without action, James said our faith is dead. With it, our faith can grow.

August 19
"Believe That You Have Received It"

IN ADDITION TO A proper perspective (see "Daily" from three days ago), persistent prayer (see "Daily" from two days ago), and applying works to our faith (see yesterday's "Daily"), another way to increase faith is to put the matter behind us. After we have done these three things (perhaps among other things) we have, in a sense, done all we can. Of course this could change. Yet another key to increasing faith is to adopt the attitude that God has now taken care of it. Thus Jesus said, "Therefore I tell you, whatever you ask in prayer, believe that you have received it, and it will be yours" (Mark 11:24). The fact that Jesus said, "Believe that you have received it" tells us that faith requires that at a certain point we treat our needs, worries, and desires as something God has already taken care of. Receiving a certain outcome is still dependent on the will of God (Luke 22:42; 1 John 5:14); preparing for the future also includes realizing that something undesirable may occur (Ps 23:4). Yet a way to increase faith is to believe that God has already taken care of a matter. This is because, among other things, to do so suggests that we realize and accept that we can do no more about it. More importantly, we have therefore finally turned it over to God. For this reason we might end this process by thanking God for having taken care of it (Phil 4:6).

August 20
"Not to Us"

ONE OF THE FUNDAMENTAL characteristics that defines worship is that it is unselfish. The psalmist expresses this essence when he states, "Not to us, O LORD, not to us, but to your name give glory, for the sake of your covenant loyalty and your truth!" (Ps 115:1). Through this psalm we are, among other things, reminded that worship is for God rather than ourselves. The psalmist also speaks of worshiping for the sake of "covenant loyalty," or being in a right relationship with God, and of "truth," or worshiping in the proper way before God. For the Christian today both of these are encapsulated in the words of Jesus, that it is necessary for us to worship him "in spirit and truth" (John 4:24). If our acts of devotion are offered "to us," they might cease to be worship.

August 21
"We Make It Our Aim"

WHILE PHYSICAL GOALS ARE good, and even necessary for a fulfilling life, the Christian can also adopt goals geared toward their spiritual life. Paul spoke of his goal of being pleasing to God: "so whether we are at home or away, we make it our aim to please him" (2 Cor 5:9). Paul's words "we make it" tell us that goals must be set; that is, if they are not given some concrete form, they are little more than an elusive dream. This verse also tells us that goals are personal ("we make it our aim") in that goals do one little good if they are adopted, for example, to make someone else happy. Paul's goal in this verse was that God would be well pleased (the Greek word translated "please" has to do with God's delight toward man, and is a different word than that used of Jesus in Matt 17:5). Paul's goal here was also in view of the judgment by God (v. 10); it was more important to Paul to please God than, for example, to please men (John 12:43). The determination that is often provoked by a goal, which for the Christian includes the ultimate goal of heaven, can keep us on the road that leads there. It can also help us know that we are well pleasing to God, which is a key factor in reaching that goal.

August 22
It's Looking Up

THE CHRISTIAN LIVES IN a world different from the non-Christian. A fundamental law of nature is that everything in the world is winding down. For the Christian, however, everything in life can rather be improving. Paul said, "And we know that for those who love God all things work together for good, for those who are called according to his purpose" (Rom 8:28). This verse tells us that things are getting better for the Christian. It does not necessarily mean that life "works" the way we define it, or that we always receive what we want. Rather that because of the Christian's love for God, and their faith in such promises as this, the Christian can know that though the world is falling apart, things for the Christian are coming together. The flesh and the Spirit are contrary (Gal 5:17). Thus, though the law of nature tells us the world is crumbling, the law of the Spirit is one of life (Rom 8:2). For the Christian things are looking up; they are working together for good.

August 23
Making Mistakes

THANKS TO ADAM AND Eve we live in an imperfect world (Rom 5:12), one in which things go wrong, and we do wrong things. After they had sinned they had a chance to come clean (Gen 3:11) but instead, among other things, they tried to blame someone else (Gen 3:12–13). While sin and other imperfections are a negative element in life, they can be an opportunity for good if we respond accordingly (2 Cor 12:9–10). If we are responsible for the wrong, we find ourselves at a crossroads (Prov 17:3; 22:3). It can be, especially if it's our fault, a moment in which we admit our wrong, ask for forgiveness, and in the process strengthen our relationship with God and perhaps with others. Mistakes are going to be made; the primary good that can result depends on whether we grow spiritually therefrom (whether it be forgiveness, 2 Sam 12:13; learning, Prov 26:11; becoming stronger, Heb 11:34; etc.). It's a lot better than blaming someone else.

August 24

"Looking to Jesus"

WHERE WE LOOK CAN affect our mood, outlook, and motivation. To "behold the lamb of God" (John 1:29) can give us strength by, among other things, removing sin that keeps us from running a successful life race (1 Cor 9:25). When running a marathon, we can assume (for those of us who have never actually run a marathon) that the runner has to look somewhere. The Christian is to be "looking to Jesus" while running the race set before him: "therefore, since we are surrounded by so great a cloud of witnesses, let us also lay aside every weight, and sin which clings so closely, and let us run with endurance the race that is set before us" (Heb 12:1). Whether we look at the .2 miles ahead of us (a marathon is 26.2 miles), at others who didn't make it, in our mind at the pain we bear, or even at the cloud of witnesses, can either be encouraging or discouraging. Our main focus is to be on the One who walked the path before us (1 Pet 2:21) because, among other things, he has reached the finish line, wherein lies the prize for which we strive (Phil 3:14). To keep looking to him gives us both endurance and motivation to complete the arduous task ahead of us, that of reaching that prize.

August 25
Unacceptable Worship

A SINCERE HEART ALONE does not determine acceptable worship. Again, it is possible for worship to be rejected by God because one's heart is not right before him (Jer 14:12), or it might be rejected because the form of worship is incorrect (even though the heart is sincere). Worshiping incorrectly might stem from worshiping something that does not exist (like the prophets of Baal, 1 Kgs 18:20–29), worshiping the true God with false teaching (Matt 15:8–9) or worshiping with unacceptable offerings (Mal 1:8). A sincere heart does not automatically convert an incorrect act of worship into a correct act of worship, any more than a sincere heart would cause an act of sin to be acceptable to God. If worship is (partly) for the purpose of drawing our heart closer to God's heart, such a process is expedited by our heart being more like his, in that we conform our will to his will, that is, according to his word. If we do, the form of worship will be that which God desires, and will be born of a heart that desires to give it.

August 26
"Seek First"

ONE OF THE KEY lessons in Jesus' command to "seek first the kingdom of God and His righteousness" (Matt 6:33a) is that of making the kingdom a priority. If we are active in life we are going to put something first, which means that other things are not going to be first. To choose to seek God's kingdom first may be easy (at first) depending on the condition of one's heart. The more difficult aspect may arise when we realize that in so doing we are making other things wait. To not, for example, give prior attention to one's work, family (Luke 14:26), or their own personal enjoyment because they are seeking first the kingdom requires strength. We can overcome this fleshly weakness by using spiritual strength (Matt 26:41) to do the right thing. We often give the most attention to the temporal things of life such as making a living (not that this is necessarily wrong). To recall Jesus' promise that the things we work for will be added to us (Matt 6:33b) can give us the spiritual strength to overcome the desire to make God take second place. God can give us both the strength to do the right thing, as well as the sustenance that we need to continue so doing (2 Cor 9:10).

August 27

"Grace and Knowledge"

SINCE THE BIBLICAL CONCEPT of grace is defined as God's unmerited favor (when we deserve punishment), how can Peter command Christians to "grow in the grace and knowledge of our Lord and Savior Jesus Christ" (2 Pet 3:18; the word "grow" is a command in Greek)? This would be like a child telling their friend to get more presents on their birthday. Perhaps it is because the phrase "grace and knowledge," which appears only here in the NT, is to be understood as a unit (like the phrase "odds and ends"). Grace being a favor means that it can't be earned (Rom 11:6); Paul said we certainly don't acquire more grace by sinning (Rom 6:1–2). Yet Christians do control how they spend their mental energy; we can and should therefore increase our knowledge of God's word. Even if it be only by "odds," the "ends" could be more grace.

August 28
Seek First by Being First

SEVERAL VERSES OF SCRIPTURE teach that, with regard to receiving help (a response) from God, we are to make the first move. God does not change (Heb 13:8), and he is always willing to help (Luke 11:10–13). Surely what is best for us is not simply to receive gifts (or even help), but that which is best for the soul, i.e., our spiritual good. Several verses contain commands that are followed by a promise. Some examples include Jer 33:3, "call to me so that I may answer you"; Luke 6:38, "give, and it will be given to you"; and Ps 37:4, "and take pleasure in the LORD, so that he would give you your heartfelt requests." Implied in each is that the promise won't be fulfilled unless and until we take action. Seeking first the kingdom includes making the first move.

August 29

Talents and Growth

CHRISTIANS HAVE A RESPONSIBILITY both to use their talent(s) and to grow spiritually. Talents are qualities that are given to us (or with which we are born), and that God expects us to use as good stewards (Matt 25:14–30; 1 Cor 4:2). We also have the responsibility of growing in Christ, the result of which will be the qualities of spiritual fruit (Gal 5:22–23; see Mark 11:12–14). Both, therefore, are not something over which we can necessarily glory in ourselves, but rather are areas we should use to glorify God (Eph 1:12). Imagine if one used more energy to both applying their talent and to growing in Christ, how much more would they be? Or rather, how much more would God be glorified?

August 30

"That the Scripture Might Be Fulfilled"

AN UNFULFILLED MESSAGE CAN be a distressful thing. Imagine receiving a call from a lawyer telling you that you stand to inherit a lot of money, that they would explain more later, yet "later" never came. The NT is the fulfillment of the Old. Of the many blessings the Christian receives as a result of Jesus' death, one is that it points us to Scripture. This is because Jesus' death is spoken of as the fulfillment thereof. Several verses reflect this idea, including Luke 18:31: "And taking the twelve, he said to them, 'see, we are going up to Jerusalem, and everything that is written about the Son of Man by the prophets will be accomplished'" (also John 19:28, 36; 20:9). Jesus' death as the fulfillment of Scripture tells us that God's plan is now complete, that God has provided everything necessary to save us, and that our acceptance of the gospel will mean our forgiveness. Jesus' death, among other things, pointed us to the word that saves our soul (Jas 1:21). God fulfilled his promise; it is up to us to accept it to receive our inheritance (1 Pet 1:4).

August 31
Not This, But That

MANY TIMES SCRIPTURE TEACHING has the effect of turning conventional wisdom on its head, or offering the opposite of what one would expect. For example, several times in the Sermon on the Mount Jesus said, "You have heard that it was said . . . but I say to you" (Matt 5:21–22, 27–28, 43–44), and when one needs money, the worldly mind naturally thinks that the answer is to get more money. Jesus said, however, "Give, and it will be given to you" (Luke 6:38). Also, while the natural way of treating an enemy is to respond as they might to us, the NT teaches to do them good (Matt 5:43–44) instead of taking vengeance on them (Rom 12:20). This is not to say that doing the opposite is to be the automatic answer to every situation; how to apply which biblical principle surely depends on several factors. Yet these things reflect Scripture teaching that the natural is the opposite of the spiritual (1 Cor 2:14). The Christian does not live as the worldly minded. Having been converted from this world and its way of thinking, and living according to principles that are often contrary to this world, the Christian can know that life works for them in a different way (Rom 8:28), and that they are going to a place opposite that of this world (1 Pet 1:4).

September 1
My Teaching

THE BEGINNING OF THE school year has always been for many an exciting time. Education is important for the proper development of the mind for both young and old. Education is also spiritual, inasmuch as thought affects the heart and soul, and the heart and soul affect the heart. What makes a good teacher, student, and parent (Col 3:21) is therefore ultimately spiritual. It is important for all of us, whether an active student or not, to be careful of the input into our and our students' minds. There are both good and bad influences around us (people, search engines), some of which are unavoidable (1 Pet 5:8). If we as Christians keep the Bible first (Deut 6:6–9), and guard that which influences our own thoughts, we can do a lot to preserve the purity of our soul, which is more important than any degree or career. We may not be able to control such powerful external things as the weather, but we can control something more powerful and more important, that is, our mind. How we educate our mind (Col 3:2) through our thoughts (Phil 4:8), and the source of our input (Rom 12:1–2) can determine the quality of our spiritual life.

September 2

Putting Away

WHEN ONE PUTS ON Christ (Gal 3:27), or the "new self" (Col 3:10), they have in process put off the "old self" (Col 3:9). Several other verses address the Christian's apparent need to put things off after they have become a child of God. Some things in life are difficult to get rid of, like something clinging by static to a garment. Some things we want to hold onto (such as a secret vice), though we know we should let it go. Maintaining a pure soul often requires a deliberate putting off of negative elements (that is, they often don't go away by themselves). Thus the Bible mentions a need to do away with things that might either cling to us or that we might be tempted to carry: the Christian is to "lay aside" sin (Heb 12:1); to "put away" falsehood (Eph 4:25); to let "bitterness, wrath," etc., "be put away" (Eph 4:31); and to "put away" childish things (1 Cor 13:11). Good things in life generally must be sought for, are more difficult to achieve, and require more energy and diligence to maintain; the things that are not as good for us are generally easier to acquire. One day we will involuntarily "put off" this earthly tent in which we live (2 Pet 1:14). If we are to be donned with a better garment (Rev 19:8) we must be ready by making sure we are rid of negative things that might be clinging to us—or to which we might be clinging.

September 3
Somebody's Going to Win

WITH REGARD TO THE outcome of the game(s) of life, the only real certainty is that someone is usually going to win, and someone is going to lose (though no one really knows which). Victory and defeat are part of playing a game. Though the pain of defeat can be a fearful thing, the possibility of victory can be a good motivator. The Bible speaks of the Christian's "overcoming" such things as evil (Rom 12:21), the world (1 John 5:4), and death (1 Cor 15:55). The Greek word translated "overcome" is related to the Greek word *nike*, which literally means "victory." In the world evil often seems to be winning; yet Jesus assures that he has already won (John 16:33), and therefore Christians will overcome. Even though our struggle is ongoing, and we can certainly lose a battle (Eph 6:13), if we hold to our faith, we are assured of being "more than conquerors" (Rom 8:37). Through faith the eternal outcome is already certain: faith is the Christian's victory.

September 4

To Be Able

When tempted, our goal as Christians should be the spiritual victory of overcoming, rather than succumbing, to the temptation. Perhaps more important than a single victory is the spiritual development one might gain by resisting. When speaking of resisting temptation, Paul said, "No temptation has overtaken you that is not common to man. God is faithful, and he will not let you be tempted beyond your ability, but with the temptation he will also provide the way of escape, that you may be able to endure it" (1 Cor 10:13). The twofold purpose Paul gives at the end of the verse is that the Christian "may be able to endure." The Greek word translated "be able" is again related to the Greek word for *power*. Perhaps our way of escape is, like Jesus (Matt 4:1–11), to look to God's word (the power, Rom 1:16) to overcome temptation. Rather than fleeing (as Satan will, Jas 4:7), to avail oneself of the way of escape can provide the Christian the means of gaining power, as by so doing they can not only have a single victory, but thereby develop their spiritual life toward greater spiritual victories.

September 5
"This I Will Call to Mind"

HOPE AND DESPAIR ARE both conditions of the mind, and therefore ultimately spring from knowledge, whether true or perceived. The confident expectation of hope with regard to the future is something, therefore, one can control. The writer of Lamentations (Jeremiah) spoke of how his recall gave him hope: "This I will call to mind, therefore I will hope" (Lam 3:21; the Hebrew literally reads "this I will return to my heart; therefore I will hope"). To return something to the heart suggests a knowledge that perhaps had left, that the writer recalled in his mind. Paul spoke of providing knowledge for the purpose of giving hope and avoiding sorrow (1 Thess 4:13–18). Harboring knowledge from God influences the heart for spiritual good (Phil 4:8), while being ignorant of God can contribute to despair. Jeremiah was in process of lamenting the downfall of his city. He overcame his despair by recalling a knowledge of God. The despair of outward circumstances can be overcome by recalling in our heart the knowledge of God, if the knowledge of God is there to begin with.

September 6

"How Can We Sing?"

SINGING IN WORSHIP IS for a purpose. Worship by definition is for the purpose of praising or glorifying God. Its effect, however, can be to uplift the worshiper, just as one who helps someone else up a mountain finds themself at the top of the mountain. Thus Christians are told to sing "one to another" (Eph 5:19; Col 3:16). It may be difficult to sing under difficult circumstances (the psalmist asked, "How can we sing the song of the LORD on foreign soil?" Ps 137:4). Yet difficult circumstances need not keep us from singing (Matt 26:30; Acts 16:25), and can even help us by reorienting our minds from ourselves toward God. Even though this may not be why we sing, and we can sing out of jubilation (Jas 5:13; compare 1 Sam 2:1) as well as under adversity, to concentrate on the primary spiritual purpose of singing in worship can help our soul move upward toward God by uplifting him.

September 7

Keeping Memorial

MEMORIES CAN BE BENEFICIAL to the extent to which we use them to affect the present. Whether it be the memorial of service men and women who fought so that others can be free of government tyranny, the memorial festivals that God wanted his people of old to keep (Exod 12:14), or the Christian today keeping the Lord's Supper "in remembrance" (1 Cor 11:24), a memorial is established so that the living can be affected for some positive (spiritual) good. To keep memorial is therefore a responsibility on the ones keeping it. When we think on the past we tend to remember the positive things. Part of the good effected thereby is by remembering that sometimes "negative" action is necessary to produce good for the present (for example, to recall a former state of enslavement [Deut 5:15; 1 Pet 2:16] can positively heighten the freedom one now enjoys). The effort expended in keeping a memorial alive is worth both the preservation of the memory as well as the resulting positive spiritual good.

September 8

"Grow"

THE CHARACTERISTIC OF GROWTH is an indication that something is alive. Having been made spiritually alive (Eph 2:5), the Christian is then told to grow. Peter said, "But grow in the grace and knowledge of our Lord and Savior Jesus Christ. To him be the glory both now and to the day of eternity. Amen" (2 Pet 3:18). The command to grow is also a reminder that the Christian can never stop giving attention to spiritual things. That is, growth is not a job to be completed, and thus is a command seemingly never fulfilled. One's attitude as a Christian should then be to concentrate on this never-ending obligation, rather than looking forward to finishing the task of growing. We can do this in part by maintaining a desire for the word for the purpose of growing (1 Pet 2:2). It is good to have a goal we can never reach. Otherwise we might stop too soon, which should make us question our being alive in Christ (Rev 3:16).

September 9

The Reward of Rest

LIKE FOOD, PHYSICAL REST can be both pleasurable and practical. Since humans were ordained to work (Gen 2:15), physical rest can serve the purpose of rejuvenation so that one can return to work (Mark 6:31). On the other hand spiritual rest, or stopping our work for the Lord, seems to be something for which the Christian must wait. That is, like the matter of spiritual growth (see yesterday's "Daily"), spiritual rest seems to be another unattainable goal while the Christian is living this life. Hebrews 4:9 reads: "So then, there remains a Sabbath rest for the people of God." Neither work nor physical rest should be an end in themselves. The Christian will receive the reward of rest at the end when there is no more work to be done (2 Thess 1:7). In the meantime, to be consistent in our work for the Lord (1 Cor 15:58) can help ensure our faithfulness to the Lord, and therefore to finally receive the reward of rest to which we look forward (Heb 4:11).

September 10

Energy to Carry On

CHRISTIANS ARE TO USE their energy to bring glory to God (Mark 12:30; Col 3:17). Even though our energy will one day come to an end (2 Cor 4:16), we need energy to continue in this life. The way one lives their physical life can affect their spirit, and the attention one gives to their spiritual life can affect their body and thus their energy level. A misuse of the body (such as sin, 1 Cor 6:19–20) or the mind (such as a lack of faith which contributes to stress) can diminish the energy level and, more importantly, affect the soul. A proper treatment of the body, such as sleep (Mark 6:31; Ps 4:8), or exercise which profits little (but does profit, 1 Tim 4:8) can contribute to a healthy mind, and therefore to the well-being of the soul. A strong spiritual life can give one physical strength. Isaiah 40:31 reads: "But those who wait for the LORD will renew (their) strength; they will raise their pinions like the eagles; they will run and not become weary; they will walk and not become faint" (Isa 40:31). Giving proper attention to a spiritual life by such means as prayer, Bible study, etc., can give one energy to carry on, until the time this body runs out of energy, and the spirit goes home to rest with God (Rev 14:13).

September 11

"Every Day Let Me Bless You"

IN PS 145:2 THE psalmist expressed his unending desire to worship God: "Every day let me bless you, and praise your name forever and ever" (Ps 145:2). In poetic words, the psalmist is expressing his heartfelt desire to worship God, to the point that he seems to want to do so continually. The Hebrew phrase translated "for ever and ever" here means for an indefinite period; this was its basic meaning in the OT, and it is here parallel to the phrase "every day." The psalmist begins the psalm with expressions of his personal desire to praise God (the word "I" is reflected six times in vv. 1–6, yet the psalmist makes no other references to himself until v. 21); so he ends the psalm in v. 21 with a similar desire to praise God forever as an individual, while at the same time inviting everyone to do the same: "my mouth will speak the praise of the LORD, and all flesh will bless his holy name forever and ever." From the NT perspective, the psalmist's language in v. 2 serves as a reminder that the Christian today who engages in consistent worship as part of a right relationship with God will one day praise him for all of eternity (Rev 5:13–14), in other words, "for ever and ever."

September 12

Scripture Works

HAVE YOU EVER TURNED to the Scriptures trying to find an answer to a specific problem in life? This can be a good thing to do. Yet, since the Bible does not read like an instruction manual for assembling a new bookcase, we might say that learning and dwelling on Scripture rather contributes to a strong spiritual life, which can help us with problems in other ways. In addition to other spiritual activities such as prayer, dwelling on Scripture contributes to the positive development of our soul, with promises such as the material things of life being added to us (Matt 6:25–34), and things working together for some good purpose (Rom 8:28). Like a planted tree (Ps 1:3), the one who meditates on Scripture is more likely to have stability to endure life's problems rather than fix them directly, and to produce fruit in due season. If we make dwelling on Scripture our goal, our specific problems may or may not be fixed; but our spiritual life will be stronger, and this is one of the most practical things we can do.

September 13
"The" Purpose of Being Humbled

AGAIN, JESUS TAUGHT THAT we are going to be humble. One either humbles themselves after which they will be exalted or, if they exalt themselves, they will be humbled (Luke 14:11). While we are told that God resists the proud and gives grace to the humble (which verse appears three times in Scripture, Prov 3:34; Jas 4:6; 1 Pet 5:5), we are not given in these verses a purpose for being humble(d). Yet, the pain of being humbled, like any discipline, would seem to benefit one's soul if or when one learns something therefrom. That is, while the lessons to be gained from being humbled may be myriad, one might learn such things as how to gain spiritual strength (2 Cor 12:10), how to grow closer to God and, perhaps most importantly, how to be humble. Following the example of Jesus (Matt 26:42), if we humble ourselves God will exalt us (Phil 2:6–9; 1 Pet 5:6). Whatever the ultimate purpose of our being humbled (if there is but one), the bottom line is that this is what God wants, rather than what we want. Maybe that's the purpose.

September 14
To Be and Not to Be

THE CHRISTIAN IS TOLD in Scripture to be, to become, and not to become certain things. Some of these include being strong (Eph 6:10), watchful (1 Pet 5:8), following a good example (1 Cor 11:1), and becoming like others for the purpose of influencing them for the gospel (1 Cor 9:22). Christians can also be subject to negative influences around them. The Bible warns that "evil communications corrupt good morals" (1 Cor 15:33), and that one must be careful not to let themselves "be conformed to this world" (Rom 12:2). We thus have the choice of being or becoming something good, or letting ourselves become something not good before God. Like keeping a garden free of weeds, keeping our health up as best we can, or anything else good, this requires effort. By giving attention to a proper spiritual life, we can thereby guard against the negative influences that are liable to corrupt our soul, rather than having a healthy spiritual life through which the Christian can become what God wants, and one day be like God (1 John 3:2).

September 15
No Worries

OUT OF ALL OF your current problems, if someone offered to fix one for you, and thus make the worry go away, which one would you choose? Does it ever seem we enjoy worrying (or that we would be uncomfortable if we had no problems)? Jesus' teaching against worry reminds us of the destructiveness of worry, inasmuch as worry contributes to both our physical as well as our spiritual detriment (Matt 6:25–33). Other Scriptures indicate the Christian's need to avoid or overcome worry, to the point that we are taught "in nothing be anxious" (Phil 4:6 ASV), and to cast our anxieties on him (1 Pet 5:7). While God doesn't necessarily offer to fix any of our physical problems, he has given us a spiritual solution to the problem of worry by directing us to overcome worry through the spiritual means he has provided (in between the lines, it is possible for a Christian to have a myriad of physical problems yet not have any worries). That is surely something we can live with; or, put another way, worry is something the Christian should live without.

September 16

"Go Worship"

WORSHIP, AS DESCRIBED IN the Bible, is something we go and do. That is, it has a specific purpose, as opposed to a job we mechanically check off, or something like pleasant music we leave playing in the background. Some examples include Abraham telling his young men that he and Isaac would "go a ways and worship" (Gen 22:5), and the eunuch from Ethiopia had "come to Jerusalem to worship" (Acts 8:27). Other Scriptures that speak of Christians' coming together, and what we are to do when we come together (1 Cor 11:20), show that worship is again a deliberate activity in which the Christian engages. God needing nothing from us (see Ps 50:12–13) does not mean that worship can be treated like any other activity (online or otherwise). When we read in the Bible of others being told "worship God" (Rev 19:10), combined with other Scripture teaching, it reminds us that if we give the act of worship a special place in heart, and thus in our schedule, it will fill a special place in God's heart.

September 17
Our Spiritual Identity

BEING ABLE TO PROPERLY identify someone or something is important (such as recognizing a poisonous plant, or the issue of identity theft in our present time). Before God gave the Ten Commandments he began with an assertion of his identity: "I am the LORD your God" (Exod 20:2). Our physical appearance helps us recognize each other, most even using physical appearance as the basis for making a judgment. God, however, sees us differently (1 Sam 16:7). We are also told today that while appearance helps identify, it is not the basis for judgment (John 7:24). The Christian is God's possession (1 Pet 2:9; Acts 27:23), inasmuch as God recognizes their spiritual identity (Rev 14:1). Such things as our outward appearance, our occupation, and our possessions (Luke 12:15) we will one day leave behind (1 Tim 6:7). That which will remain is our spiritual identity, that by which Christ will recognize us (or not, Matt 7:23) in the end. Do you see what I mean?

September 18

"Ears That Hear Not"

MANY THINGS, FROM A "stiff neck" (Acts 7:51), to accepting fables (2 Tim 4:4), to simple rebellion can keep one from accepting truth. God said through Ezekiel that his people had rejected his word because of their rebellious heart: "Son of man, you live in the middle of a rebellious house, who have eyes to see, but they have not seen; ears to hear, but they have not heard; because they are a rebellious house" (Ezek 12:2). In contrast to the idols they worshiped, who were said to have eyes and ears, but were unable to see or hear (Ps 115:5), God's people had functional eyes and ears; but what prevented them from recognizing and acting upon God's word was their heart. That is, they could have obeyed, but their rebellion prevented them from accepting God's word. Rebellion, like most rejection of truth, boils down to selfishness (or self-interest). Truth by definition does not change. Rather than changing the message to suit our ears, the best thing we can do is to change our heart (Acts 2:37) so that we accept the unchanging truth. If truth, for example, grates on the ears, we change that not by changing what we hear, but by changing how we hear it (Luke 8:18). We change our ears, and thus accept God's word, by changing a (perhaps) rebellious heart.

September 19
"If You Know"

KNOWLEDGE ALONE CAN BE beneficial or harmful, depending on the kind of knowledge, There may be a false message which satisfies the ears but is destructive to the soul (Jer 6:14; 2 Tim 4:3), or a true message that distresses the soul (Hab 3:16). Truth, and therefore a knowledge of it, sets free (John 8:32). Yet Jesus said that, in effect, knowledge imposes a responsibility: "If you know these things, blessed are you if you do them" (John 13:17). While any knowledge may impact the soul, one's action based on that knowledge is how the knowledge is fulfilled. Work alone is not the answer, but the best plan is useless without our putting it into action. God would have us to know the truth (2 Thess 2:12), then mentally process it through reason (Isa 1:18) toward an understanding of God's will, which would ultimately culminate in action such as expressed in Acts 2:37: "Now when they heard this they were cut to the heart, and said to Peter and the rest of the apostles, 'Brothers, what shall we do?'"

September 20
Forgetting the Past

A KEY INGREDIENT IN being able to carry on in life is to not let oneself be encumbered by the past. While remembering certain things can be beneficial (Deut 5:15), forgetting certain things is also necessary. A key in this regard is how this knowledge spiritually affects us. Paul said, "Brothers, I do not consider that I have made it my own. But one thing I do: forgetting what lies behind and straining forward to what lies ahead" (Phil 3:13). We have a choice upon what our mind dwells. While we may or may not be able to delete information of the past (the Greek word translated *forgetting* in other contexts has the idea of "neglecting"), we can overcome the past in part by both dwelling upon positive things (Phil 4:8) and by not dwelling on things we should leave behind. Not that recalling the past is necessarily a sin; but being able to leave it behind is surely a key factor in our being unencumbered to face the future, and to run free to Jesus (Heb 12:1–2).

September 21

"A Cheerful Giver"

WHEN THE CHRISTIAN APPROACHES God in worship, one of his first concerns should be with whether God will be pleased with the worship he offers. As we have noted, both the manner of worship and the condition of the worshiper's heart determines whether our worship is acceptable to God (John 4:24; Amos 5:21). Since Paul said that "God loves a cheerful giver" (2 Cor 9:7), we should therefore want to be cheerful when engaging in the giving portion of worship (the reverse of this statement is that God does not love, or he rejects, an uncheerful giver). Inasmuch as love "does not insist on its own way" (1 Cor 13:5), a key to being a cheerful giver is surely the attitude of unselfishness. When it comes to each of us parting with our own money (1 Cor 16:2), the attitude of our heart should be a desire to please the One to whom the money is directed rather than ourselves. If our heart is desirous of keeping the money, this could reflect a selfish heart, and therefore suggest an attitude in which God does not take delight. Rather, if we engage in worship from a heart conditioned by love, it will provoke the love of God in return, as we offer worship acceptable to him.

September 22

"Summer Is Ended"

THE HARVEST SEASON, ESPECIALLY for those who live directly from the land, has always been a joyous time. This is the anticipated time when much-needed food supplies are gathered at the end of the season, and the farmers are left with an abundance of produce to sustain them until next year. Jeremiah 8:20 reads, "Harvest has passed, summer has ended, and we for our part have not been saved" (Jer 8:20). This verse in context indicates that the spiritual decline of the nation had resulted in physical calamity. A spiritual application of this verse today reminds us that whatever we will be blessed with later depends both on the seed we sow now (Gal 6:7), the diligence with which we tend to our crop (1 Cor 3:8), but will result in a joy that does not depend on physical substance (Hab 3:17–18). By walking "in the light" (1 John 1:7) the Christian can know that their life will produce fruit (Gal 5:22–23), and thus not disappoint the Lord (Mark 11:12–14). When our season of life comes to an end, at the time we need it most, we can expect to be saved (1 John 5:13) and thus have joy at harvest time.

September 23
Increasing in Strength

AN ATHLETE IN TRAINING who increases their strength is, over time, still running out of energy. Strength is seemingly always an admirable quality. Spiritual strength can supplement physical endurance (Isa 40:31), even while our physical strength is generally diminishing (2 Cor 4:16). Yet the Bible says that the new convert Saul (Paul) "increased all the more in strength, and confounded the Jews who lived in Damascus by proving that Jesus was the Christ" (Acts 9:22). The phrase "increased . . . in strength" is one word in the original Greek, and from which is ultimately derived the English word *dynamite*. Though this verse doesn't say what this strength is, the entire context has to do with Paul's work in the word (see vv. 20, 29; and the result in this verse was that he was to disarm his opponents with argumentation). The gospel is the power of God (Rom 1:16). The Christian is told to be strong (Eph 6:10), through such means as grace (2 Tim 2:1), faith (and thus the word of God, Rom 4:20; 10:10), and, more generally, "through Christ" (Phil 4:13; each of these verses contains the word under discussion). While some of these verses do not define this strength, it is fitting that, like Paul, an increasing knowledge of the word increases our spiritual strength. Combined with other aspects of a strong spiritual life, absorbing God's word on a regular basis (see Ps 1:1–3) contributes to our spiritual stability, and even increasing strength, in the midst of a life of physical weakness.

September 24
Love as Acceptance

ONE WAY THE WORD *love* (or its opposite, *hate*) in the Bible can be understood is as acceptance (or rejection). Love is of course a very complex emotion (the ancient Greeks had four words for it). This is not to say that it bears this meaning in every passage in the Bible; but to think of it in this way can help us understand the possible meaning in several verses (see also our "Daily" of Sept. 21, where we suggested that the reverse of God loving a cheerful giver is that he does not love, or rejects, an uncheerful giver). Some verses that seem to bear the meaning of love as "accept" and hate as "reject" include Jesus' teaching for one to "hate father and mother" (Luke 14:26); God's declaration of "Jacob I loved, Esau I hated" (Rom 9:13); and the Christian's admonition to "love not the world" (1 John 2:15). Understood this way, among other things, helps us reconcile such Scripture teachings that God can reject someone who does not obey (Matt 7:23) while still loving them (John 3:16).

September 25
The Necessity of Prayer

IT IS NECESSARY FOR Christians to pray, and often (usually?) what drives us to pray is a necessity. Jesus said that he gave the parable in Luke 18:1 "to the effect that they ought always to pray and not lose heart." The Greek word translated "the effect" bears the meaning of a necessity. While the lady in the parable evidently received what she had asked for (v. 5), Jesus' parable is given for the purpose of our "praying without ceasing" (1 Thess 5:18) by one's not losing heart. This implies that it is good for us to have something to pray about and, in between the lines, that it is good when our requests are not satisfied. Not that it is bad when they are satisfied; in 1 Sam 2:20 Eli prayed that God would bless Elkanah with a child "in place of the request" that his wife Hannah had made. If we shift the focus of our attitude in prayer from only satisfying a need or want to "thy will be done," prayer will be a much more spiritually beneficial exercise. Would you keep praying after your request is granted?

September 26

"Full of Good Works"

The Bible describes Dorcas as a woman "full of good works" (Acts 9:36). The word "full" suggests that her life was complete with regard to good works. While the extent of this expression may be open to discussion (that is, they may be open questions when one is full of good works, whether one needs to fill their life with good works, and whether one is ever done with good works), the word alone suggests completeness, that her life couldn't hold any more good works. Again, such things as prayer (Luke 18:1) and spiritual growth (2 Pet 3:18) may be said to be spiritual pursuits that are "never" completed. Could this difference be due to the fact that good works are physical? While good works are to be part of the Christian life (Eph 2:10), such an expression as this regarding Dorcas reminds us that physical things, including good works, can have fulfillment. Like qualities such as strength (Isa 40:31) and a proper mind (Rom 12:2), it seems we have a need to see to their renewal, so that we stay active in good works, anticipating the time when all things will end. Until that time we fill our lives with such things as good works.

September 27

Worship God (Again)

GOD DOESN'T NEED ANYTHING (Ps 50:12). Yet it seems, based on observation, that man has a need to worship (reflected in such things as man's behavior toward entertainment, money, and himself). Several examples (the idolatry of people throughout the Bible, as well as people's behavior in modern times) seem to reflect this evident truth. Some passages of Scripture thus contain commands in which one is told to or how to worship (Pss 136:1; 149:2; etc.). John in Rev 19:10 tried to worship the angel who gave him the message, at which he was told "worship God" (ASV; see also Acts 10:25–26). Such may reflect not only the command to worship, but also that the subjects needed to be directed what to worship. Like a child being told to take a nap, being told to do what we need in this regard again reminds us that worship should be less about what we want. Worship is an act of reverence directed toward the Creator of the universe, for the purpose of expressing our adoration in order to exalt and glorify him rather than ourselves.

September 28
Fear and Comfort

ACTS 9:31 STATES "so the church throughout all Judea and Galilee and Samaria had peace and was being built up. And walking in the fear of the Lord and in the comfort of the Holy Spirit, it multiplied" (Acts 9:31). Based on this verse, the early church lived their spiritual lives according to two concepts that seem at odds. Fear is often thought of as a negative concept; yet the "fear of the Lord" (see tomorrow's "Daily") is a scriptural principle whereby the Christian lives their life in conformity with God's will. It is consistent with the "comfort of the Holy Spirit," inasmuch as to live the Christian life is to have the comfort that only comes from a life at peace with God (Rom 5:1). Both can and should be part of the life of Christian, as living the Christian life leads to spiritual blessings, such as peace and comfort, that one can attain no other way (Eph 1:3). Just as Paul housed two things that truly were at odds (his physical "thorn in the flesh," which resulted in the simultaneous residing of the "power of Christ," 2 Cor 12:9), so the Christian can live according to the two complimentary concepts of the "fear of the Lord" and the "comfort of the Holy Spirit." Walking "in the fear of the Lord" is the means of ensuring the "comfort of the Holy Spirit."

September 29

"The Fear of the Lord"

THE BIBLE SPEAKS OF two opposite types of fear. One is a positive condition of heart, borne of love and respect, that produces an attraction toward; the other is a negative condition of heart that causes one to be repelled. The first type of fear Christians are to harbor (Matt 10:28), the other is to be overcome, as it is the opposite of faith (Rev 21:4). Acts 9:31 (see yesterday's "Daily") again states that the early church was "walking in the fear of the Lord." By walking the path that God has set for the Christian, that is fearing him as demonstrated by keeping his word (Ps 119:105), the Christian thereby can overcome, and thus walk without, the negative fear. The way to overcome the negative fear is with the positive fear. The Christian can then join with the psalmist "even though I should walk through the valley of the shadow of death I would not fear evil because you are with me" (Ps 23:4).

September 30
"The Comfort of the Holy Spirit"

IN LANGUAGE THE WORD *of* can be used to mean many things ("the running shoes of Dave"; "Liz is of California"; "George preached of salvation," etc.). When the Bible speaks of the "gift of the Holy Spirit" (Acts 2:38) this can mean either a gift the Holy Spirit gives, or that the Holy Spirit is the gift. The same is true of the "comfort of the Holy Spirit" in which the early church was said to walk (Acts 9:31; see the last two "Dailies"). The Holy Spirit is elsewhere called the "Comforter" (John 14:16). The phrase "comfort of the Holy Spirit" therefore can be understood as "the comfort of the Comforter." Christians are promised comfort from God (2 Cor 1:3–4). Without saying what this comfort is, Acts 9 (vv. 27, 29) and elsewhere in Bible (John 16:13; Heb 3:7) indicates that the word of God is a central part of how the Holy Spirit works. By walking in God's designated way, the spiritual blessings which the early church enjoyed (such as peace and being built up) can be ours today as well. We walk in a world of tribulation (John 16:33); Jesus, who has overcome the world, offers comfort through his Comforter.

October 1

"The Sacrifices of God"

THE PSALMIST STATED THAT "the sacrifices of God are a broken spirit; a heart broken and crushed, O God, you will not despise" (Ps 51:17). Again the word *of* can mean many things (see yesterday's "Daily"). In Ps 51:17 the word *of* seems to be used in the same way we would speak of a "garden of vegetables," that is, a "vegetable garden." The "sacrifices of God" may then be "godly sacrifices" (in the OT the Hebrew word translated "God" can also be used to refer to the best of something [as we would say "that dessert was heavenly"; Gen 10:9]). He states that what makes a sacrifice (worship) godly is that it is one born of a broken spirit. This would seem to be a negative thing; but it can be contrasted with such things as a haughty spirit (Prov 6:17) or a flippant attitude (Mark 12:41–44), which cause one to offer anything they want even if it is of poor quality (Mal 1:8). God will more readily accept worship today when it is born of a proper spirit (1 Cor 11:27; 14:15). The best kind of sacrifice, a godly sacrifice, is one which is offered through such spiritual qualities as love and humility, in other words, a broken spirit.

October 2

The Basis of Freedom

THE BASIS OF FREEDOM is love. Freedom, the opposite of which is slavery, is a basic desire of humans. Love, which is basically unselfish (1 Cor 13:5) is a spiritual quality which requires spiritual attention, and is therefore neglected or not understood by many. Love is the basis of a search for truth (1 Cor 13:6); thus if one loves Jesus they will follow his truth (John 14:15), which will set them free (John 8:32). Man is, after a fashion, in prison anyway (this was the ancient Greeks' view of man's physical existence), which condition is usually made worse by man's treatment of his fellow man. God offers spiritual freedom, which is not dependent on outward circumstances. Our need as Christians is to see that the spiritual light of freedom is not squelched. Truth is the means of spiritual freedom; if we love Jesus we will pursue truth, which sets us free.

October 3

It Won't Get Too Hot

As CHRISTIANS WE ARE going to have difficult times (2 Tim 3:12), including perhaps persecution. If we don't, it could suggest our lives are not distinct enough from the world (Luke 6:26). Among the many perspectives we gain from difficult times, one need we have as Christians is to be aware of the inevitability of those times, and to reflect on our spiritual strength in view thereof. God has promised that he bears the responsibility of the intensity of those trials; that is, God's scriptural promise is that the trial will not be too much for his children to bear. God will sit and watch so that the "fire" does not get too hot (Mal 3:3), and that there is no trial that we are not able to bear (1 Cor 10:13; he does not say he will remove the trial). These thoughts can help us both when a difficult time arises as well as when the trial seems to us unbearable. When the trial does seem unbearable, perhaps the answer for us is to look at our circumstances differently, from a perspective of which God would approve, that is, through the perspective of his promises—and thus endure the trial.

October 4

Look at It Spiritually

IN THE SERMON ON the Mount Jesus said, "Look at the birds of the air: they neither sow nor reap nor gather into barns, and yet your heavenly Father feeds them. Are you not of more value than they?" (Matt 6:26). To consider the physical beauty and wonders of nature can give the beholder pleasure. Such things as the ocean, the mountains, and wildlife can be both fascinating, wondrous, and therefore pleasurable to look at. Jesus' invitation to "look at" is, however, not physical, but spiritual (the meaning behind the Greek word thus translated has to do with putting thought into one's gaze). Not that it is wrong to look at nature with a pleasurable eye; but Jesus is, as it were, inviting his listeners to consider the wonders of nature from a different perspective, toward the spiritual goal of their not worrying (vv. 31–34). Imagine if we applied this spiritual perspective not just to nature, but to all of life; it might just help us with such spiritual problems as worry.

October 5
"I Have Learned"

PAUL TOOK NOTE OF his circumstances, and even used them as a means of teaching (2 Cor 11:23–27; 1 Thess 2:9). Yet Paul's (dis)comfort while on this earth seems not to have been the most important thing to him. Circumstances and conditions can certainly affect such things as our mood and even more important aspects of our being (viz., our soul). To be impoverished is a very unpleasant way to go through the one life with which one is blessed. To be wealthy is usually, however, not good, due to the effect it can have on one's soul and their relationship with God (Luke 6:24). The physical conditions of one's life are important to the extent, therefore, that they affect the soul. Thus Paul said, "Not that I am speaking of being in need, for I have learned in whatever situation I am to be content" (Phil 4:11). In Paul's mind, that which was more important than his physical circumstances was the spiritual benefit of having learned from it. Paul looked at his life spiritually and tried to teach us so.

October 6

"Wandering off into Myths"

JUST AS GOD CREATED humans without sin, so he also intended humans to live according to truth. Paul spoke of those who turn from the truth and wander off into myths: "and will turn away from listening to the truth and wander off into myths" (2 Tim 4:4). To turn from truth requires a conscious application of the mind toward myths or other error, and suggests that one can't follow both. The Greek word translated "turn away from" has a meaning of turning the direction of the ears for the purpose of not listening (and is therefore not physical but spiritual). The Greek word translated "wander off into" is used in other contexts of a limb out of joint. Just as this is not normal, and is normally painful, it can be set right. While leaving the truth is to get one's soul out of joint, one can be set right by coming back to the truth. No matter how appealing, myths, like any falsehood, are not normal. God's word is truth (John 17:17), not error; it is therefore not from men (Gal 1:10). Like a body set right, God's word sets our soul free (John 8:32), the way God had intended.

October 7

"For He Is Good"

THE PSALMIST CALLED UPON his listeners to praise God because of who he is: "Give thanks to the LORD, for he is good; for his covenant loyalty is forever" (Ps 136:1). The reason he gives for praising God is because God is good. The rest of the psalm offers reasons why God is good; that is, these things, including God's covenant loyalty, are some of the ways God's benevolence reaches us. Yet for the psalmist the first reason he gives, and perhaps the ultimate basis for worshiping God, is his essence. This again reminds us that worship is unselfish, and that being unselfish benefits us. While one becomes right with God because of what it means for them (the salvation of their soul), worship, when properly engaged in, spiritually benefits the worshiper when offered from a heart willing to part with itself and offer itself to God. God doesn't need our worship (Ps 50:10–13); for the worshiper to give thanks, or worship God, because of who He is benefits him, not Him.

October 8
Our Daily

THE CHRISTIAN LIFE IS not something that one sets up and lets run on its own; it rather requires consistent (daily) spiritual effort. Jesus said, "And he said to all, 'If anyone would come after me, let him deny himself and take up his cross daily and follow me'" (Luke 9:23). Maintaining anything on a regular basis may be a challenge due to such variables as circumstances and personal feelings. The Christian life, however, requires perpetual vigilance (Eph 5:15), among other things because Satan is always lurking (1 Pet 5:8), and Jesus could return at any time (Matt 24:36). To do this includes offering our body as a living sacrifice (Rom 12:1), reflecting the consistent effort of Paul that "I die daily" (1 Cor 15:31). If we have died to the world (Gal 6:14), our need then is to keep up our spiritual life on a daily basis by remaining dead to sin, but alive to Christ, and that daily.

October 9

"Purpose of Heart"

ACTS 11:23 STATES THAT Barnabas exhorted the early church "that with purpose of heart they would cleave unto the Lord" (ASV). The phrase "purpose of heart" reminds us both of the need to be dedicated to the Lord as well as the fact that dedication is designed in the heart. The Greek word translated "purpose" is used in reference to God's showbread as something set out in dedication to God (Matt 12:4), as well as God's purpose for those who love him (Rom 8:28, "according to his purpose"). Humans have the ability to do right or wrong depending on the direction of, and how they choose to use, their heart. One day on my morning run I saw an injured bird in the middle of the road who sadly had just been run over by a car. The bird's friends had been with him or her before their being run over and, on my return run, were still there after the bird had been killed. Such behavior in animals is borne of instinct, rather than of a conscious decision designed for moral good. Humans, however, can set their heart so that it is dedicated, with a purpose, to God. If we design our heart so that it is directed to him, he will set out a way, or have a purpose, for us.

October 10
Our Talent

EACH OF US IS given at least one talent that we are expected to use for God's glory (Matt 25:14–30). We often wish we could have another talent (such as when we observe a successful entertainer and wish we had the ability to do what they do). One reason an entertainer is successful is not because they wished they had been given another talent, but in part because they used the talent they did have. To use what we have is a reflection of good stewardship (1 Cor 4:2), is the means by which the Christian brings glory to God (Col 3:17), and is one of the keys to having a full heart in this life. To long for something else is equivalent to a child being disappointed with their gift, instead wishing they had been given something else (how does such a reaction cause the giver of the gift to feel?). Rather, the best thing we as Christians can do in this regard is to show our appreciation for our talent by being busy using what we have been given. If we do, it may be that God will give us more (2 Cor 9:10; Matt 25:29), and he will surely be glorified. Using what we have is more important than just possessing an innate ability. If we apply our ability accordingly, we may not become famous among men, but God will recognize our efforts (Matt 25:23) whether "successful" in this life or not.

October 11

"The Peace of God Will Guard"

IT IS COMFORTING ENOUGH for the Christian to know that they can have the "peace of God" (Phil 4:7) that comes from the "God of peace" (Phil 4:9). There seems to be an irony, however, when Paul speaks of the peace of God guarding the Christian: "Do not be anxious about anything, but in everything by prayer and supplication with thanksgiving let your requests be made known to God. And the peace of God, which surpasses all understanding, will guard your hearts and your minds in Christ Jesus" (Phil 4:6–7). The Greek word translated "guard" is a military term, meaning to protect or keep watch over. This implies being guarded against something. Some ancient cities, such as Jericho, had towers, but the dating of the remains in archaeological terms has left us wondering what they were afraid of; that is, the remains are so old that we can't tell who their enemies were. The Christian has enemies, such as one's own lusts (Jas 1:14), evil that could overcome us (Rom 12:21), and Satan who is constantly lurking about (1 Pet 5:8) and throwing fiery darts (Eph 6:16). Yet Paul's promise is that by not worrying and by letting our requests be made known to God, God's peace will guard us from spiritual enemies. Our enemies may go so far as to kill the body (Matt 10:28); but, being held in Jesus' hand (John 10:28) means we are protected. By worrying we let our guard down; not worrying and praying means we are guarded by the peace of God.

October 12
"There Am I"

ACCORDING TO THE NT, certain acts of worship are meant to be carried out in a group. Again, some acts of worship (such as praying) can be carried out any time, by oneself. Other acts of worship, such as communion (the very word indicates something done with others) and singing "one to another" (Eph 5:19) reminds us that some worship is corporate. We might also observe that what takes place in a group is different than when one is alone (compare the excitement one feels when watching a sporting event in a stadium with fifty thousand others versus watching it at home). For these reasons the dynamic for Christians is different in corporate worship, as it includes the fact that Jesus is with our group: "For where two or three are gathered in my name, there am I among them" (Matt 18:20). Though worship is first for God, a gathering of Christians on the first day of the week is special, as it offers something one otherwise cannot get. Just as God adds one to the church (Col 1:13; Acts 2:47), and Jesus will deliver us to God as the body of his people (1 Cor 15:24), so worship in a group serves a purpose that can't be otherwise fulfilled.

October 13
"Thy Will"

SINCE GOD DOESN'T NEED anything we have to offer (Acts 17:25), what is the one thing that makes our gift(s) pleasing to him? A gift without a giver is not a proper gift; that is, the mechanical action of sending something of value likely doesn't touch the heart of the recipient if it does not flow from the heart of the giver. Thus the Bible speaks of obedience from the heart (Rom 6:17), of sacrifice as vain when it is not from the heart (1 Cor 13:1–3) and, throughout the Bible, of doing God's will. Though both love and the will are complex emotions (and there may thus be more involved), it is our will born of love that makes our gift pleasing to God. Jesus' offering his life in the garden was pleasing to God because it was the one moment when he could have exercised his will to avoid it, but instead chose to bow to God's will in order to please him (Matt 26:42, which reads "again, for the second time, he went away and prayed, 'My Father, if this cannot pass unless I drink it, your will be done'"). Jesus did this because of his desire to fulfill God's commandments, which is an attitude stemming from a heart of love (John 14:15). A heart desirous of pleasing God is a heart of love, and is one that will ultimately lead to one's saying "not my will." For Jesus, the moment of preserving the only thing he had left in this world (his life) was the moment to let go of the one thing God seemingly wanted, Jesus' will.

October 14

One of These Days

SEVERAL TIMES JESUS TOLD the disciples things he wanted them to know ahead of time: "I am telling you this now, before it takes place, that when it does take place you may believe that I am he" (John 13:19). There were many times the disciples had trouble believing what he said (John 6:60–66). Jesus also said that those who did believe what he said were more "blessed" even though they had seen no other evidence (John 20:29). We don't know the future, and we can't always know the impact (or not) of our words, example, or life in general. Yet we do know the power of God's word (Rom 1:16). Thus, the Christian can know that their labor is not vain in the Lord (1 Cor 15:58), and that by working in the gospel they are at least saving themselves (1 Tim 4:16). Not everyone will believe in the gospel; but, this being the will of God (1 Tim 2:4), we therefore share with them the one message that can save their soul, in the hope that maybe one day they would believe. Today Jesus' message is contained in his written word (John 17:17); it stands for us to believe, partly in view of the time when that message would make sense to us. The written word does not change; yet our circumstances and, perhaps more importantly, our understanding, can.

October 15

No Matter What

A KEY TO SUCCESS, in both physical and spiritual endeavors, is to not quit, no matter what happens. To avoid quitting requires several spiritual qualities, one of the main ones being that of determination. It seems that we often decide to quit based on that which is best for us. Not that this is necessarily wrong (there will always be roadblocks in life); but, among other things, Paul taught that one characteristic of love, being an unselfish spiritual quality (1 Cor 13:4), is that it believes and endures all things (1 Cor 13:7) and that it "never fails" (1 Cor 13:8). To quit something in life is sometimes necessary (Paul gave up on people; 1 Tim 1:20); but quitting is an action which is final and is the one way to ensure that the endeavor in which we are engaged will not come to fulfillment. This being true, to not give up is necessary if we are ever to succeed. Nothing we can do will change the love of God toward us (Heb 13:5–6), or remove our saved condition with Jesus (John 10:29). As Christians our need toward God is to trust him (Ps 23:4), to serve him (Dan 3:17–18), and to follow him (1 Cor 15:58)—no matter what.

October 16
"The Time of Your Sojourning"

If we found ourselves living in a foreign country, we might have an uncomfortable life, if for no other reason than because it's not home. We might therefore spend our days harboring pleasant thoughts of home, an exercise which could both occupy and comfort our mind until we arrived home. Peter said to "pass the time of your sojourning in fear" (1 Pet 1:17 ASV). In the OT, a "sojourner" was a resident alien. This included not having the rights of a citizen, but being expected to live by the laws of the land. It also included the knowledge that one was not one of the locals (the corresponding Akkadian word carries an idea of being hostile). This reminds us again that the Christian is not a citizen of this world (Phil 3:20), and that the life the Christian lives is different from the world (Rom 12:2), since the world is hostile to it (1 Pet 4:4). Our time on earth is limited (Heb 9:27), and therefore temporary (Jas 4:14), and is therefore not to be wasted (Eph 5:16). But since we are sojourners, one can profitably spend the one life they are given in view of the better country to which they look forward (Heb 11:16). Just as Jesus looked forward to going home (John 17:11), so the knowledge that our stay on earth is temporary need not be a negative thing, but can rather serve as motivation to endure until the time we go home to be with our Father.

October 17

"I Will Sing with My Mind"

PAUL SAID THAT SINGING in worship is to be from the mind as much as from the spirit: "What am I to do? I will pray with my spirit, but I will pray with my mind also; I will sing praise with my spirit, but I will sing with my mind also" (1 Cor 14:15; several translations have "understanding" instead of "mind"). This verse serves as a reminder of the power of music to influence the mind of the singer by way of the heart. A negative illustration of this truth is the prevalence of immoral lyrics in pop music, which is concurrent with a decline in morals over the last sixty years. On the positive side, this verse reminds us that singing "psalms, hymns, and spiritual songs" (Eph 5:19; Col 3:16) with the mind as well as the spirit can positively affect our spiritual life. Just as we engage in prayer with our mind, a similar effect can be gained by concentrating on the words we sing. Singing praise to God has an intellectual as well as an aesthetic function, both of which can draw us closer to God while we offer this "fruit of our lips" (Heb 13:15) in praise to him.

October 18

"Not Conformed"

TWICE IN SCRIPTURE (ROM 12:2 and 1 Pet 1:14) the Christian is told not to "be conformed" to this world or to sinful ways: "do not be conformed to this world, but be transformed by the renewal of your mind, that by testing you may discern what is the will of God, what is good and acceptable and perfect" (Rom 12:2). The Greek word thus translated appears only in these two verses in the NT, and has the idea of shaping something into a mold. The word is also passive, which suggests that it is something done to us. Evil is an active force which would like to squeeze the Christian into its mold. They may not be able to change what we are (modeling clay in the shape of a doughnut still can't be eaten). The Christian is rather to conform their image to be like God's Son (Rom 8:29; the word "conform" there being a different Greek word), something the world can't change no matter how hard they squeeze.

October 19

Keeping God's Word

WHY IS THE BIBLE esteemed highly by some but not by all (by the same token, why are some books revered over the Bible)? The psalmist stated: "How would a (prestigious) young man purify his way? By keeping (it) according to Your word" (Ps 119:9). The meaning of the Hebrew word translated "keeping" is surely wide-ranging (each modern version consulted translates it differently). Yet, as the seed which is alive (1 Pet 1:23) and gives life (Jas 1:21), the word can nevertheless be snatched away (Luke 8:12), we could drift away from it (Heb 2:1), or otherwise neglect it. Rather, by doing such things as regularly meditating on God's word (Ps 1:2), and keeping it in one's daily life (Deut 6:4–9; Heb 5:12–14), God will surely keep watch over his child who so keeps his word.

October 20

"Preparing Your Mind"

PETER SPOKE OF THE Christian's preparing their mind for action: "Therefore, preparing your minds for action, and being sober-minded, set your hope fully on the grace that will be brought to you at the revelation of Jesus Christ" (1 Pet 1:13). The phrase "preparing your minds" is in Greek literally "girding up the loins of your mind." This has reference to one in ancient times binding their clothing around their waist to allow greater mobility. Peter here speaks of three actions: preparing the mind, being sober-minded, and setting one's hope. We might view each of these in terms of different possible events: preparing the mind suggests the need to be ready for something that we anticipate (like a student preparing for a test); being sober-minded is an attitude the Christian adopts as part of their spiritual way of life (1 Thess 5:4–8); and having our hope set on Jesus' return is a positive attitude of expectation toward something that has not yet happened (1 Thess 4:13–18). Inasmuch as a threefold cord is not easily broken (Eccl 4:12), the Christian who adopts these three perspectives could possibly be ready for anything.

October 21
Designed to Be Active

A FRIEND OF MINE who runs for exercise told me that he believes our bodies are designed to be active. The Bible describes the Christian life as both a "walk" (Eph 4:1; Col 2:6) and a "run" (1 Cor 9:26; Heb 12:1). We might wonder how both can be true; yet, as these are both figures of speech, the two images in general tell us that the Christian is to be active in their spiritual life. One emphasis throughout the Bible is on how we are to do each (for example, "walk worthily," Eph 4:1, and "run with patience," Heb 12:1). Yet, be spiritually active we must. Being physically active is good for us (1 Tim 4:8) and may be a necessity; being spiritually active is a necessity and is also good for us. Humans were designed to be spiritually active.

October 22

"The Meditation of My Heart"

Worship being something that is offered first for God may make the worshiper wonder how they can know whether their worship is pleasing to God. The psalmist said, "May the words of my mouth and the meditation of my heart be acceptable before you, O Lord, my Rock and my Redeemer" (Ps 19:14). The Christian today can know that their worship is pleasing to God by the teaching that has been delivered. Regarding the Lord's Supper Paul said, "For I received from the Lord what I also delivered to you" (1 Cor 11:23). Paul said he "received" this teaching (see 1 Cor 15:3), meaning that he received it from God (see to the contrary Gal 1:12), which he then "delivered" to the Corinthians (1 Cor 11:2). This stands as inspired teaching for us today to follow (1 Cor 14:37), and thereby we can know that observing the Lord's Supper is an act acceptable to God. Having been delivered to us, we therefore keep it to make our worship, or the meditation of our heart, acceptable in God's sight.

October 23

"These Things Will Be Added"

When we recall Jesus' teaching in Matt 6:33, "but seek first the kingdom of God and his righteousness, and all these things will be added to you," we often (properly) emphasize such things as the word "first." We can also observe that there is a difference between the words "seek" and "added." The word Jesus used with regard to the kingdom ("seek") is active, while the word used of the physical benefits we will receive ("added") is passive (as also reflected in the original Greek). Certainly one must do their part in providing for themselves and their family (1 Tim 5:8), and Christians (are to) make the best employees (Col 3:23). Based on Jesus' teaching in this verse, a key element in the Christian life is that we can be passive with regard to physical things; thus, even when striving to make a living (physical), we could still be seeking the kingdom (spiritual). If we be active in pursuing spiritual things first, we can be passive in pursuing physical things because God is actively providing them for us.

October 24

I Can't Wait

TIME CAN BE LOOKED at as a precious gift from God who created it. As such, Christians ought to cherish this gift by making the most of it. Unlike many gifts, this one is going to go away no matter the extent to which we make use thereof. Thus Christians are told to make the most of their time (Eph 5:16), since today is the only day they have. Paul said, "For he says, 'In a favorable time I listened to you, and in a day of salvation I have helped you.' Behold, now is the favorable time; behold, now is the day of salvation" (2 Cor 6:2). To hope expectantly for tomorrow is of course not wrong, unless our hope is ultimately placed in something other than God (1 Pet 1:21), or we harbor a negative attitude such as anxiety (Phil 4:6). Since today has enough trouble of its own (Matt 6:34), it is good for Christians not to be always wishing that tomorrow would arrive. The past can serve many things, including happy memories, and a desire for tomorrow can provide anticipation that can motivate us to good things. Yet today is the only time we have. Looking at it as a gift from God can help us make the most of this favorable time.

October 25
Wait for It

MANY TIMES IN LIFE a decision has to be made on the spur of the moment. For these times preparation is one of the best lines of defense (Phil 4:8). Some decisions, however, need not be made immediately. Proverbs 21:5 states, "The plans of the diligent surely lead to plenty, but one who is hasty will surely come to poverty." Based on this verse, a good suggestion with regard to making some decisions (those on which we can wait) is that we make ourselves wait on purpose. To take this approach may offer several benefits, including that it allows us time to ponder the situation from every angle (that is, to let wisdom germinate). Yet the primary benefit for the Christian is the time this affords us to pray. In between the lines, it also tells us that not having what we want, and even having problems, can be a good thing (as Paul spoke in 2 Cor 12:9–10). If we take this approach it may or may not help us with our problem; but it will give us an opportunity to draw closer to God. If we make a decision too hastily, it likely will not.

October 26

"Let Your Light Shine"

JESUS TAUGHT FOR US to let our light shine (Matt 5:16), but not to do our righteousness to be seen of men (Matt 6:1). It seems that both can be true when they are looked at according to their purpose. To do things for others to see is evidently motivated by a desire for the glory of men (Matt 6:2). It also may be that we have to choose which glory we desire (John 12:43). Christians are rather to do good works for others to see (Phil 2:15), and thereby bring glory to God (Matt 5:16). It seems that it is difficult to keep a source of light hidden (1 Tim 5:25). The reason we let our light shine can be either proper or improper, depending on the effect we hope to achieve when it shines on others (such as those living in darkness, Matt 4:16). We don't do it so that the light will hurt their eyes, but that it might reflect positively on the Source of light (Gen 1:3) and thereby lead them out of the darkness.

October 27
"Draw Near to God"

JAMES'S EXHORTATION TO DRAW near to God is a general teaching on improving one's spiritual life: "Draw near to God, and he will draw near to you" (Jas 4:8). While James doesn't give any details (such as how to draw near to God), it seems we can apply this injunction to the specific area of worship, among other things. Surely drawing near to God begins with one's spiritual life (Eph 2:8–10). Physical proximity to God is not possible (1 Kgs 8:27), because God is a spirit (John 4:24) who is far above us (Isa 55:9) while at the same time near to us (Acts 17:27). Yet the Christian can think of drawing closer to God in worship as a means of strengthening their relationship with him. Through communion with one's spiritual brothers and sisters (1 Cor 11:20–29), heartfelt songs and prayers (1 Cor 14:15), by which (prayers) we approach God's throne with our petitions (Heb 4:16), we can know thereby that God is drawing near to us. What better way to face the physical life with its difficulties than with a strong spiritual life, attained by leaving the world and drawing near to God in worship?

October 28
"God Is Able"

WHEN PAUL SPOKE OF God being able (Eph 3:20), he described the extent to which God can work in the life of the Christian: "now to him who is able to do far more abundantly than all that we ask or think, according to the power at work within us." Paul also said that God's word is able to build us up (Acts 20:32), and that Paul would glory in his weaknesses so that the power of Christ would rest upon him (2 Cor 12:9). Not that God is ever unable to do anything; yet, in these verses Paul teaches that God's "ability" to work in the life of the Christian is dependent on the Christian's weakness and, perhaps more importantly, on the extent to which the Christian turns that weakness into strength by relying on God's power—God's word.

October 29

"Resist the Devil"

THE CHRISTIAN CAN WIN over evil both by doing good (Rom 12:21), and by not doing evil. Not doing evil includes resisting evil. James said, "Resist the devil and he will flee from you" (Jas 4:7). As in the physical realm (such as weight training), resisting evil requires strength to carry out. The Christian can get this strength from the primary source of power, God's word (Rom 1:16). He or she can then be equipped to stand against Satan (Eph 6:11), like Jesus who resisted the temptations of Satan by using God's word (Matt 4:1–10). Though this requires strength, and may make us tired (see Matt 4:11), it can in the long run make us spiritually stronger. If resistance does make one spiritually stronger, surely not resisting makes us spiritually weaker.

October 30

"I Commend You to God"

SEVERAL TIMES IN SCRIPTURE we read of someone "commending" someone to God (or something similar). This word (also translated "set before" or "commit") bears a sense of setting someone or something before another, like we recommend someone for a job. It therefore has a sense of entrusting to another. It appears in the NT of setting food before someone (Mark 6:41; 1 Cor 10:27); of setting Scripture before the hearer for their consideration (Matt 13:31) or obligation (2 Tim 2:2); and of one's committing their spirit (Luke 23:46) or soul (1 Pet 4:19) to God. Only once in Scripture is the word used of entrusting someone to both God and to Scripture. In Acts 20:32 Paul said to the elders of Ephesus, "And now I commend you to God and to the word of his grace, which is able to build you up and to give you the inheritance among all those who are sanctified" (Acts 20:32). As Paul was about to leave these fellow-Christians whom he loved, he entrusted them not only to God, but to God's word, that which is entrusted to Christians for their salvation.

October 31
No Place for the Word

UNDERSTANDING SOME CONCEPTS (FOR example, physics) may be difficult for the non-expert. Other times understanding something is simply a matter of giving the concept a chance. Jesus said to the Jews that their desire to kill him was because "my word finds no place in you" (John 8:37; he also said in v. 43, "Why do you not understand what I say? It is because you cannot bear to hear my word"). The Greek word translated "find (no) place" in v. 37 is used in other contexts of there being enough physical space (Mark 2:2; John 21:25), to one making room in their heart for spiritual concepts such as repentance (2 Pet 3:9). Sometimes understanding someone or something is simply a matter of being open to giving someone's words a chance in our heart. To do so can cause a light to go on in our mind, and thus (depending on the concepts entertained) possibly lead one to the truth. To keep the door of our heart closed (Rev 3:20) may make us feel secure; but if we make no room for the truth we can never be free (John 8:32).

November 1

What's in It for Me?

WHAT DOES THE WORSHIPER get from engaging in the acts of worship? In short, what we get is that we get to give. In general, what attendees do when they come to worship has changed through the years, yet church attendance generally is said to be in decline. Again, worship is by definition unselfish compared to such things as entertainment. The acts of worship the Christian is to engage in today (prayer, singing, 1 Cor 14:15; the Lord's Supper, 1 Cor 11:23–29; giving, 1 Cor 16:2; preaching, Matt 15:9) are intended first to please God. By offering these things from the heart, the worshiper can thereby hope to please God rather than himself. If we do, what we get in return is that we are blessed by, and in proportion to, what we give (Acts 20:35; Luke 6:38).

November 2

"It Would Throw Truth to the Ground"

TRUTH DOES NOT CHANGE, but it can affect or change the hearer in different ways. Like a light shining on one in darkness for the first time, truth can be refreshing or uncomfortably blinding (Matt 4:16). Since Jesus is truth (John 14:6), what one does with the truth after knowing it can be a reflection of their ultimate attitude toward Jesus. In one of Daniel's visions he saw a horn increase in power, to the point that it "would throw truth down to the ground" (Dan 8:12). Casting something to the ground can be a sign of contempt or rejection. The Christian is to have such a high regard for the truth that we (the church) uphold it for all to see (1 Tim 3:15). When others hear truth they might turn their ears from it (2 Tim 4:4) or stop their ears to avoid hearing it (Acts 7:57). It is possible for one's words to drop in a positive (Ezek 20:46) or a negative sense (1 Sam 3:19). But we are to uphold the truth regardless, lest it be taken by others and thrown to the ground.

November 3

"You Have Been Grieved"

It seems that one reason more people do not do the right thing is because it can be difficult. The fact that Paul taught the Christian to "stand," after having taken up the spiritual armor in preparation (Eph 6:10–18) tells us, among other things, that standing for the right may be difficult, and may produce pain either for ourselves or for others. While we also don't seek pain in life, choosing the easiest way (for example, telling a lie to avoid hurt feelings), is not necessarily the answer either. Thus Peter taught: "In this you rejoice, though now for a little while, if necessary, you have been grieved by various trials" (1 Pet 1:6). Since pain is part of living in this world, in many situations (such as leaving a job) somebody is going to be made unhappy. To do the right thing for spiritual reasons means the Christian endures pain for a little while, knowing that a greater benefit awaits. If we don't so stand it might spare someone some pain; it will also, however, likely grieve the Holy Spirit (Eph 4:30, the Greek word translated "grieve" is the same as in 1 Pet 1:6). How much better that we be the ones grieved by doing the right thing.

November 4

"The Genuineness of Your Faith"

WHILE THE CHRISTIAN IS enduring trials it is good to remember both that he or she does so for a purpose, and that he or she does so again under God's oversight. Thus Malachi said, "So He will sit (as) a smelter and purifier of silver; and he will purify the sons of Levi and refine them like gold and silver, and they will be the LORD's, those who bring offerings in righteousness" (Mal 3:3). Among other things, this verse tells us that God will not let the crucible in which the Christian is being tested become too hot. Testing can serve the purpose of purifying our faith toward the end of glorifying God (1 Pet 1:7) and, toward that end, God has provided a means by which we can escape (1 Cor 10:13). These verses do not tell us what the outcome of our testing will be. Like the apostles of old, some tests may claim our lives. Yet, rather than take from us our precious faith (John 10:28), tests can rather serve to make our faith stronger and more pure. And, perhaps more importantly, bring glory to the One overseeing our trials.

November 5
That's No Excuse

THE NATURAL WORLD IS of course a wonder to behold. Such things as the beauty of the parrot fish, a beautiful sunset, or the dance of bees to communicate to their friends are marvels to consider. Yet utilizing our eyesight need not be only a physical exercise, but can also be a spiritual exercise. That is, one can look at these things for different reasons, just as we look at life, problems, or the future from a different perspective. We might say that there are only two ways to look at the physical world, either with a physical perspective or with a spiritual perspective. Paul said that God's natural world is evidence of spiritual things: "for his invisible attributes, namely, his eternal power and divine nature, have been clearly perceived, ever since the creation of the world, in the things that have been made. So they are without excuse" (Rom 1:20). The Greek word translated "without excuse" means that the one in this verse has no reason to justify their behavior. Not that it is necessarily wrong to simply appreciate beauty; yet one can look at the beauty, design, and grandeur of the world through physical eyes and draw one conclusion. Or he can look at the physical world through spiritual eyes and be impressed with the fact that all of this beauty and design exists because of a Designer. The existence of these things leaves us without excuse in drawing such a conclusion.

November 6

How's It Going?

GIVING IS AN ACT of worship, the proper fulfillment of which depends on how one's life is going. With regard to giving Paul taught "on the first day of every week, each of you is to put something aside and store it up, as he may prosper, so that there will be no collecting when I come" (1 Cor 16:2). While other aspects of worship may also be affected by how our personal lives are going (such as suspending worship in order to make things right with a brother, Matt 5:23–24), the act of giving our money to God is based on the extent to which we "prosper." This spiritual rule is not a financial guideline (we are not given, for example, a percentage by which to determine the precise dollar amount). One can rather use this Scripture teaching as a spiritual principle to help them draw closer to God through this particular act of worship. Perhaps if we engage therein properly, as we should every act of worship, and thereby give in such a way that it pleases God, our worship will affect our lives (Luke 6:38).

November 7
Three Things Lacking

THE PROPHET HOSEA SPOKE of his countrymen as having lost three important aspects of their spiritual life. He said, "There is no truth, nor covenant loyalty, nor knowledge of God in the land" (Hos 4:1). In the OT context, truth is the basis of covenant loyalty, or that concept on which Israel's spiritual life as a nation was formed. To keep covenant loyalty made them as a people to be right with God, or to have a knowledge of God (Jer 31:34). For the Christian today, truth is the basis of the gospel (that is, the gospel is true, yet there are many truths besides the gospel, John 17:17), one's obedience to which results in knowledge of, or being right with, God (1 John 2:3). Our fundamental need is to seek truth, which will ultimately lead to one's being right with God. Israel had been given prophets like Hosea to tell them they were not right with God; unlike Israel of old, the only warning we will receive today is the gospel that God has already given.

November 8

The Power of Words

Two passages in the book of Acts that show us the power of words are Acts 15:24 and 32. Verse 24 contains a rather negative observation: "since we have heard that some persons have gone out from us and troubled you with words, unsettling your minds, although we gave them no instructions," while v. 32 is positive: "and Judas and Silas, who were themselves prophets, encouraged and strengthened the brothers with many words." While we live in a video age, words are still one of the most powerful tools at our disposal for influencing the human heart. Although v. 32 includes that they used "many words," this is not necessarily to say that the more one talks the more encouraging they are. But words have the power either to unsettle the mind or to encourage and strengthen the heart. God's word has the power to save our soul for all eternity (Rom 1:16; Jas 1:21). Whether it be on paper, digital, or when the preacher or reader arises to share God's word, we should listen because words, and especially God's word, are powerful.

November 9

Ordained and Delivered

IN ACTS 16:4 WE read that the teaching given by the apostles was both "ordained" and "delivered": "and as they went on their way through the cities, they delivered them the decrees to keep which had been ordained of the apostles and elders that were at Jerusalem" (Acts 16:4 ASV). This being the first inspired writing in NT times, these two words tell us of the importance of the letter, and that due to its teaching. The Greek word translated "ordained" has a legal meaning related to making a decision, and the Greek word translated "delivered" suggests something that has been entrusted to another. Paul used the same Greek word translated "delivered" in 1 Cor 15:3 regarding the resurrection: "For I delivered to you as of first importance what I also received: that Christ died for our sins in accordance with the Scriptures" (1 Cor 15:3). While we don't have any of the original physical NT documents today, the decision of the divine Lawgiver has been passed along to us. Not only are Christians bound to follow this law, but it has been delivered to us so that we might keep it, use it (Heb 5:14), and pass it along to others (2 Tim 2:2).

November 10

"Holy Adornment"

The psalmist said, "Worship the Lord in holy adornment" (Ps 96:9a; ESV "splendor of holiness"). The Hebrew phrase translated "holy adornment" is an expression of how we dress on the inside when we come before God to worship him. The Hebrew word translated "adornment" is used of the king in Prov 14:28; everywhere else in the OT it is used with regard to the public worship of the Lord. While God surely appreciates the effort one makes to look nice when gathering together for worship, it is the inside that God truly considers (1 Sam 16:7). This is a garment all can put on to look nice inside when coming to worship God. We do this by living a holy life according to God's word (1 Thess 2:10–13). One can become holy by putting on Christ (Gal 3:27), then continuing to be holy by wearing the garment that makes God happy to see them coming to worship—"holy adornment."

November 11

"They Knew Not the Scripture"

THE PHYSICAL EVIDENCE GOD has provided has left man without excuse for believing in him. Yet Jesus urged us toward something beyond the physical in our search for truth. In John 20:29 Jesus said to Thomas, "Have you believed because you have seen me? Blessed are those who have not seen and yet have believed." This principle is seemingly emphasized in John 20:8–9, where we read that John saw the empty tomb and believed, the reason given that "for as yet they did not know the Scripture, that he must rise from the dead" (RSV; some translations read, "they did not understand the Scripture" [ESV; NASB]). The empty tomb was the evidence they needed; these verses tell us either that they hadn't yet put two and two together and/or, as it applies to us today, that we have the Scriptures that Peter didn't. God has not asked us to believe anything for which he hasn't given sufficient evidence necessary for us to believe. We can't physically see the empty tomb today; and it's a good thing, because God has given us his word that we might believe.

November 12

"He Put a New Song"

THE PSALMIST WAS GLAD not only to sing to God, but the reason for his being able to sing to God; he thus credited God accordingly: "And he put a new song in my mouth, a song of praise to our God. Many will see and will fear, and will put their trust in the LORD" (Ps 40:3). When we are happy we often feel like singing (Jas 5:13), and in the OT a new song was used on special occasions as a means of praising God (Ps 33:1; 96:1, etc.). The psalmist is saying not just that his heart is in such a condition that he feels like singing, and that it is a blessed enough time that it calls for a new song (as Exod 15:1), but that these conditions have caused him to look to God. Thus he sings, the ultimate purpose of which is that it will cause others to trust God, or that they will also look to him. If so, it may be that he will put a new song in their mouth (and so on).

November 13

Onward and Upward

WHEN DO WE REACH the goal of having acquired enough knowledge, especially with regard to spiritual things? Peter begins his second epistle speaking of knowledge (2 Pet 1:5, 6, 8, 12), and ends his epistle with an encouragement to grow in knowledge (3:18). One of the effects of learning Scripture is that it causes us to realize how much don't know. With regard to understanding God's will, the Christian is not working toward the completion of a set of facts, as one would a college degree, but rather is to be engaged in an ongoing pursuit of knowledge whereby we grow closer to him. Following Deut 6, the Christian today is to love God (v. 5), so that he or she keeps God's word (v. 6), and that always. Verse 7 thus reads, "You are to impress them upon your children, and speak of them when you sit in your house, and when you walk in the way, and when you lie down, and when you arise." One can reach the goal of growing in knowledge by never ceasing to learn God's word.

November 14

Calling Evil Good

TO CALL SOMETHING THE opposite of what it really is can be dangerous. To convince oneself that bears in the wild are friendly can lead to one's harm or destruction. God through his prophet said, "Alas (to) those who proclaim evil good and good evil, (who) set darkness for light and light for darkness, bitter for sweet and sweet for bitter!" (Isa 5:20). The Hebrew word translated "woe" means it is going to be bad for them (the word again represents a wailing sound). The ultimate reason this is a bad thing is not necessarily because it will result in harm, but because it represents their leaving the truth (v. 24 states they have rejected the law of the Lord). Even if everything goes their way in life, one will ultimately pay a price for not recognizing what evil really is. It will be bad for them, no matter what they call it.

November 15

Motivated to Be Motivated

MANY THINGS CAN MOTIVATE us to action. The Bible speaks of encouragement (1 Thess 5:11), exhortation (Rom 12:8), and Christians provoking one another to love and good works (Heb 10:24). Sometimes external stimuli can provoke us toward good actions; sometimes, however, it seems we lack something inside that causes us to be motivated (that is, it sometimes seems that we can't get moving no matter what happens to us from outside). Just as we need something to hope in, we often need a reason to want to be hopeful. Thus, for the Christian, we may want to be motivated to do better, but not know where to find a source of motivation. Jesus is the one with the words of eternal life (John 6:68), words that can spiritually build us up (Acts 20:32). The word won't do it for us, however; we need to have a spark in our heart that can ignite a flame of motivation, and which will direct us toward God's word that gives us hope. We need to be motivated to be motivated; God is the ultimate source.

November 16

"Fear Not"

THROUGHOUT SCRIPTURE ARE CONSTANT reassurances to the child of God that God's got this. We naturally worry over the future, partly because we don't know what is going to happen. If a goal for the spiritually minded is to develop faith (which it should be), which circumstance would cause our faith to become stronger, knowing or not knowing the future? Not knowing the future provides us with a choice of either fear or faith. In Joel 2:24–27 God tells his people what he's going to do, but he begins by telling them what he's done (as if the things he's going to do have already been assured) and thus not to be afraid: "Fear not, O land; rejoice and be glad, for the LORD has done great things!" (2:21). God wants us to believe that he has already taken care of the thing we are worried about (Josh 6:1; Mark 11:24), which we can then use as a basis for overcoming fear with faith (Exod 14:13). For Israel, one goal was so that they would know that he is God (v. 27). For us the goal can be not so much to get what we want (Jas 4:3), but to develop faith by choosing it over fear. As with Israel, God thus reassures us that he's got this (Rom 8:28); and thus he tells us as well not to be afraid (Phil 4:6–7).

November 17

"Honor the Lord"

FAIRLY EARLY IN THE book of Proverbs, the wise man instructed the young person to "honor the LORD out of your wealth and out of the first of all your produce; so that your storehouses would be filled with plenty, and your vats would overflow with new wine" (Prov 3:9–10). The Hebrew word translated "honor" has to do with bringing glory to (and is the same word used of measuring wealth). Both wealth (perhaps savings) and income (firstfruits) are for the purpose of bringing glory to God rather than ourselves (1 Cor 4:1). The Christian today is to give as he has prospered (1 Cor 16:2), with the same promise that God will provide him with proportionate blessings in return (Luke 6:38). The extent to which God blesses us materially is up to him ("storehouses" and "new wine" are to be understood by Christians today as figures of speech for God providing). Whether we become wealthy in life today is up to God's will; if we do increase in substance we are to glorify God with such blessings, a responsibility God has left up to us to fulfill.

November 18
Grace to Help Us"

CHRISTIANS ARE TAUGHT TO approach God's throne for the purpose of receiving help: "Let us then with confidence draw near to the throne of grace, that we may receive mercy and find grace to help in time of need" (Heb 4:16). In this verse, that which drives us to God's throne is our "time of need," suggesting a physical or other kind of problem for which we seek a solution. Yet that which is offered in return is the spiritual quality of grace, born of God's mercy. Both of these are undeserved spiritual blessings from God (1 Tim 1:13), including as part of our salvation (1 Pet 1:3). To be given grace may not necessarily mean a resolution of our physical problem. God's answer to Paul's problem was not physical, but grace (2 Cor 12:7–10). This in turn gave Paul the spiritual quality of power (seemingly related to the gospel, Rom 1:16). It may be that we are to approach God's throne in prayer so that we take away not necessarily something physical, but something spiritual. That is, we might receive help from God in the form of grace, reinforced, at least in part, through "the word of his grace" (Acts 20:32).

November 19

Together in Unity

For relationships to be strong they must have something to tie them together. It is possible to be together yet not be united. The greatest quality which can make relationships strong is spiritual (such as worship) versus physical (such as fun times). Whether it be brethren worshiping together, a family praying together, or a nation bound by spiritual principles (Prov 14:34), it is the spiritual, versus the physical, that ultimately keeps us together and fosters our own healthy spiritual life (1 Pet 3:7). The psalmist stated, "Here, how good and pleasant (it is) for brethren to dwell even in unity" (Ps 133:1). Fun times are good, in that they provide us with us such things as happy memories; a spiritual focus provides us with a foundation for ourselves and those with whom we share such things, and that can be gained in no other way. Just as truth sanctifies (John 17:17), so by adhering thereto we can be united together, the ultimate expression of being God's people (John 17:20–21).

November 20

Bearing God's Word

MANY ARE UNABLE TO handle the truth. Whether it be due to immaturity (John 16:12; 1 Cor 3:2) or sin (Amos 7:10), we sometimes are not able to bear God's word. In Amos 7:10 Amaziah the priest said that the land was "not able to bear (Amos's) words." Some are open-minded to hearing God's word (Acts 17:32), while others, as we have noted, will cast it to the ground (Dan 8:12). More than once God told his prophets not to "drop" their message on a people that were unable to bear it (Ezek 20:46; Amos 7:16). Like a structure or a vehicle that is built to withstand up to a certain capacity, we can prepare to receive God's word by having a "readiness of mind" (Acts 17:11) by which we can receive it. God's word will not return to him void (Isa 55:11), and his word has been completed for all to receive if they will (Jude 3). Whether it be by three by five cards, a phone, or through our head, God has dropped his word on us that we might bear it in our heart. Letting it fall to the ground is a bad thing; the reason why that is, that we were not able to bear it, may be worse.

November 21

Rejoicing in Grief (or "I've Seen Worse")

DEPENDING ON THE CIRCUMSTANCES, being exposed to and preparing for bad things generally can help us prepare for worse things (Ps 23:4). There is, of course, the very serious matter of trauma, and the lasting negative effects it can have on the mind. Yet Peter states that the Christian is "guarded" through faith toward salvation (1 Pet 1:5), and that "in this you rejoice, though now for a little while, if necessary, you have been grieved by various trials" (1 Pet 1:6; the Greek word translated "guarded" is the same word Paul used of the peace of God guarding the heart of the Christian in Phil 4:7). The Christian's spiritual life gives them the means and a reason for their spirit to rejoice, even while their outward circumstances may cause them grief. By enduring outward grief through faith, one's faith can become stronger. So that, perhaps with the next trial, he can say, "I've seen worse."

November 22

"This Do in Remembrance"

MEMORABLE EVENTS THROUGH WHICH we live can serve a spiritual purpose to the extent that they (we let them) affect our soul. Past events, and therefore days of remembrance, can affect us when we recall them for a similar purpose. When we purposely recall and dwell upon past events, whether positive or negative, it is important not only to remember what was done but why. That is, it is good to remember the action, the motivation behind the action, and the meaning with which we are left. The Christian's weekly memorial of Jesus' death on the cross has meaning because of what was done (he died on the cross), as well as why (for our sins). Thus the Christian engages in an action with meaning: "this do in remembrance" (1 Cor 11:24). Knowing these two things, and what Jesus' death means for the life of the Christian, can help them use what would be an otherwise negative event in order to bring them closer to God, and to tell others of this event and its meaning (1 Cor 11:25–26). These things are true only if we remember.

November 23

The Goal of Seeking

SEEKING GOD SHOULD BE everyone's goal. While certain things about a spiritual life have a conclusion, many do not; our spiritual quest on this earth may never end. Thus Paul said that God did certain things for man "to seek God, if then they might indeed try to feel for him, and might find him" (Acts 17:27a, author's translation). Paul states that the real goal (or the first goal) is seeking, with the ultimate goal of feeling for and finding God. That is, the last two things depend on one's seeking him. Seeking is therefore a goal in itself (Matt 6:33; 7:7), and finding God does not necessarily mean we are to stop looking for him. As in many other things in Scripture and in life, if we emphasize the purpose, the end result could take care of itself. Thus we should never stop pursuing the goal of seeking.

November 24

"Occupied with the Word"

AFTER PAUL LEFT ATHENS and arrived at Corinth, the Bible speaks of his being completely occupied with his preaching and teaching: "When Silas and Timothy arrived from Macedonia, Paul was occupied with the word, testifying to the Jews that the Christ was Jesus" (Acts 18:5). This comes two verses after the Bible tells us Paul had the avocation of tentmaking (v. 3). The Greek word translated "occupied" has a basic meaning of being held together. In this verse it means that Paul was completely absorbed with his preaching and teaching, seemingly as if he couldn't help it (elsewhere it has to do with being constrained by something, Phil 1:23). Not everyone today can devote their entire life to teaching God's word. Yet Christians can be preoccupied with the word, as we devote our mind and heart to understanding it and to living it (Ezra 7:10). If we do, we might find ourselves like Jeremiah who, when he said he wouldn't speak in God's name anymore, found that he couldn't help but speak it (Jer 20:9). We are both limited to (1 Pet 4:11) and limited by the powerful word of God, because we can't help it.

November 25
There for God

As a father, God wants a relationship with his children. Unlike an operating system, that we assume is going to work but does not receive much attention on a daily basis, God desires that we talk with (1 Thess 5:17), commune with (1 Cor 11:23–29), obey, and thereby get to know him (1 John 2:3–4), though we can't see him (1 Pet 1:8). For these reasons it is good for us to have desires (Ps 37:4), problems (2 Cor 12:10), and positive resolution of problems (Luke 17:16), to impel us to speak with our Father, whom we otherwise might take for granted. As a father, God is longing for his wayward children to come home (Luke 15:20), not only so that they will be taken care of, but because of the relationship that has been missing since they left him. God is there if we need him (Deut 4:7); we should be there for God.

November 26

"The Ungrateful and Evil"

GOD HAS A GENERAL providence from which every type of person benefits (Matt 5:45). The thanksgiving holiday reminds us of the importance of being grateful in return for God's many blessings. Jesus' words in Luke 6:35 are a bit striking, inasmuch as he couples the word "ungrateful" with "evil": "but love your enemies, and do good, and lend, expecting nothing in return, and your reward will be great, and you will be sons of the Most High, for he is kind to the ungrateful and the evil." Why did Jesus choose the word "ungrateful" to accompany the word "evil"? Giving thanks is perhaps not the same as being thankful (it is possible for an evil heart to carry out a good act, Matt 7:11). Since "good" and "evil" are set forth in the Bible as two different paths, to not be grateful, therefore, suggests one has a heart pointed in the direction of evil. Thus the Bible admonishes Christians to let their requests to God be submitted with thanksgiving (Phil 4:6), and to give thanks in everything (1 Thess 5:18); there is no season for thanksgiving. To be thankful suggests a heart that is desirous of reciprocating for another's graciousness (the Greek word translated "thankful" is related to the Greek word translated "grace"). The heart can't go in two directions in life; being thankful arises from a heart that is on the path of good.

November 27

The Object of Our Worship

WHEN PAUL SPOKE IN Athens he said to his audience that his spirit was provoked within him (v. 16) as he "passed along, and observed the objects of your worship" (Acts 17:23 ASV). Paul took this opportunity and the feeling that arose within him to preach to them about the true God. It seems that for an activity to be defined as worship requires that it have an object. Again, by contrast, entertainment is generally directed toward the one observing the activity; that is, entertainment is designed for and directed toward the one being entertained. The object of worship is on the other end of the activity. To worship the true God requires that we worship in truth (John 4:24), which means that we do so according to his will (versus our will, or making ourselves the object of worship, Col 2:23). When one engages in the acts of worship today according to the NT (prayers, singing, giving, etc.), they spiritually benefit therefrom, but they are not directed toward themselves. Even the Athenians realized that their worship was directed toward something other than themselves, even if it was an "unknown god" (v. 23). To worship God properly today is assisted by our recognition that when we worship Someone is listening, because he is the object of our worship.

November 28

Overcoming Sin

SIN IS DIFFICULT, AND yet easy, to overcome. Sin (or evil) is pervasive enough that a small amount can influence otherwise pure surroundings (Gal 5:9). It is also powerful enough that it can overcome one (Rom 12:21), and persistent enough that it often can't be hidden from (Num 32:23). Yet, with a little faith (Matt 17:20), strength to resist (Jas 4:7), and effort in doing good (Rom 12:21), sin can be defeated. We can know what faith is through God's word (Rom 10:17), we gain strength from a diligent spiritual life, which includes attention to God's word (Acts 20:32), and we know what good is because of God's word (Gen 1:31). If we have God's word as the constant influence upon our soul, the pervasiveness of sin can be overcome both within ourselves and in the world.

November 29

Conscious and Conscience

PETER SAID THAT IF the Christian suffers wrongfully, they are approved by God if they take it with the right attitude: "For this is a gracious thing, when, mindful of God, one endures sorrows while suffering unjustly" (1 Pet 2:19). The word translated "mindful" comes from the Greek word meaning to have in mind (it ultimately comes from the Greek word for "idea"). The word is used most often in the NT of the conscience, or having one's heart right (the different translations of this verse show that the word can mean either). Jesus is with us as Christians (Matt 28:18–20). Part of knowing that our heart is right, or that we have a right conscience, is keeping him with us in our mind, or being conscious of him. A good conscience alone does not make us right with God (Acts 23:1); but a right conscience, as well as being conscious of God, is important to knowing that God is with us when we need him most, such as when we suffer injustice. To overcome such evil as injustice the Christian therefore has a twofold line of defense, being conscious and a good conscience.

November 30
"I Will Arise"

WE ARE GOING TO fall (fail) in life, but failing does not mean one is a failure. More important than falling is determining to rise again. Falling is easier than trying again, because it requires less energy. Micah 7:8b reads, "Even if I have fallen, I (will) have arisen; though I sit in darkness, the LORD is my light." This wording expresses both an expectation that one will fall, but also that he is prepared to overcome the fall by getting back up (both verbs are in the past tense). The prophet is also expressing his conquering fear ahead of time (Ps 23:4), and purposing in his heart to have the strength necessary to keep going (Dan 1:8). He didn't say he was going to succeed, but that he would arise. There will be setbacks in life, the overcoming of which begins in our attitude. Like Jesus who "fell" by his death on the cross, he arose, never to fall again. And, like Jesus, and because of Jesus (1 Cor 15:20), the Christian can stare down the ultimate enemy of death (1 Cor 15:55) by determining to have arisen.

December 1

"I Hate Your Feasts"

IT IS POSSIBLE FOR worship to be delightful to us but repulsive to God. While there can be many reasons for this, a primary reason is an improper life on the part of the worshiper. Such things as a poor relationship with (Matt 5:23–24), or other ill-feelings toward, one's fellow (1 John 5:20), or other perhaps general spiritual improprieties (1 Cor 11:27) may cause God to be displeased with what we have to offer. Thus in Amos 5:21 God states, "I hate, I despise your feasts, and I take no delight in your sacred assemblies." The reason given is because of the injustice that was rampant in the land at that time (v. 24). This verse contains two words translated "despise" and "take no delight," yet the general description in this and following verses is one of "hate," again meaning "reject" (the Hebrew word translated "despise" can also mean "reject"). For our worship to be accepted by God requires on our part a heart that is reflective of the spiritual qualities God would be pleased to accept; that is, a heart conditioned by such things as justice, love, and righteousness, based on God's word. Then we can know that God would be pleased with, or accept, our worship.

December 2

Mustering Up Faith

SOMETIMES IN LIFE THE hardest part of achieving something big is the first small step. Jesus said that faith as small as a mustard seed is the necessary first spiritual step to greater things: "He said to them, 'Because of your little faith. For truly, I say to you, if you have faith like a grain of mustard seed, you will say to this mountain, "Move from here to there," and it will move, and nothing will be impossible for you'" (Matt 17:20). The fact that Jesus compared the amount of faith to a mustard seed (as if to say "even this small amount") suggests that it can be difficult for some to muster up belief in God. While the reasons for this may be many (including perhaps that they would rather rely on themselves), a "tree of righteousness" (see Isa 61:3; Mark 4:32) will only grow if we plant the seed. Though it may be difficult to make this choice, at the same time it only requires a small amount of faith to overcome a mountain of fear. Mustering up faith is the moment we choose to set our heart and mind on Jesus over other attitudes such as worry. We must muster up faith, however small an amount.

December 3

One Verse

IN MATT 4, JESUS overcame each of Satan's attacks with a verse of Scripture. With each temptation Satan threw at Jesus, he countered with one verse of Scripture, thereby defeating Satan. As noted in yesterday's "Daily," even the smallest amount of faith is powerful to remove something as large as a mountain (Matt 17:20). Since faith comes by hearing the word of Christ (Rom 10:10), even one verse is powerful to overcome a spiritual challenge such as temptation. To echo the words of Paul, God is able to do "far more abundantly than all that we ask or think, according to the power at work within us" (Eph 3:20). If Jesus can overcome with just one verse, imagine what God can do with us, in us, and through us, when we fill our hearts and minds with his word. He might do more than we can imagine.

December 4

Credit or Blame?

WHEN THINGS GO WRONG in life it seems we often blame the wrong person, usually the easiest target (as we have previously noted). Many public figures are blamed for things they did not do, and many are never held to account for wrongs things they did. Justice means that one will be held to account for their actions; in the Bible we will have to answer for the life we've lived (2 Cor 5:10). In like manner, while people are quick to blame God when life does not go well (meaning that it does not go their way), the Bible teaches our need to credit God for good things (Ps 65:9–13). It seems to be naturally easier to concentrate on the negative; thus it's easier to blame God when life does not go well than it is to give him credit when it does. Though it may be difficult to know why things happen in life, to have this attitude is a way for the Christian to concentrate their positive mental energy on God at pivotal moments in life. In the words of Paul, to think on the positive includes the things that are "just" (Phil 4:8) even if it is difficult; or "in everything give thanks" (1 Thess 5:18) whether life seems just or not. In other words, don't be too quick to blame God.

December 5

The Substance of Hope

ALTHOUGH SWANS SING AS they fly off to die, it seems that animals are unable to contemplate the future. God has given man the ability to contemplate the future, with the capacity both to picture what he does not want to happen (worry), as well as what he does want to happen (hope). Hope that is meaningful is based on a real reason to expect that something could happen; even then, however, the realization of the hope remains to be seen (Rom 8:24). The Bible defines faith as the assurance of that in which we hope: "Now faith is the assurance of things hoped for, the conviction of things not seen" (Heb 11:1). Faith, or God's word (Rom 10:17) is the reason man can have a hope that, among other things, helps him overcome worry. Without faith our imagining the future could be equivalent to believing in a dream which, upon waking, one finds was not real. Such promises in God's word of his providing for our needs (Phil 4:19) and an existence with him in a place of no pain (Rev 21:1–4) are the foundation upon which the Christian's hope is based. By believing in God's word Christians have a substance that makes their hope real. We may not know when we will die, but a substantive hope gives us a reason to face the future with a song.

December 6

"The Silver Is Mine"

MORE THAN ONCE GOD reminds us that he doesn't need the offerings we bring in worship. In Ps 50 it seems the people were bringing their sacrifices to God (v. 8), yet God reminds them that he already owns everything (vv. 9–11), and thus he doesn't need it (v. 12–13). In Hag 1 they were neglecting the rebuilding of the temple and, therefore, the worship of God. So God reminds them that he already owns the money they are keeping for themselves: "'The silver is mine, and the gold is mine,' is the pronouncement of the LORD of hosts" (Hag 2:8). God doesn't need the substance we bring. He "needs" us to worship, because this is what we need. This is because, among other things, worship is unselfish. We have a need to take care of ourselves (1 Cor 6:19–20) and those in our lives (1 Tim 5:8); yet we also need to seek first God's kingdom (Matt 6:33). Our money belongs first to God, and we are stewards thereof (see 1 Cor 4:2). If we have this attitude the latter six days of the week, it will be easier to part with it on the first day of the week when we bring it to the One who owns it in the first place (1 Cor 16:2). The money is his, even though he doesn't need it.

December 7

"The Lord Heard It"

THROUGHOUT THE BIBLE WE read of God's people pleading with him to hear them (Ps 61:1), that God is able to hear us (Isa 59:1), and that false gods are not (1 Kgs 18:27). It is interesting, therefore, when we read in Num 12:2 that "the LORD heard it." This verse appears in a context of some complaining about Moses's marriage. There may be a place for a legitimate complaint (such as to solve a problem within an organization). Yet we can say that complaining (or "grumbling") against God is misplaced due to God's infallible nature. That is, if we don't like something, including the way our life is going, the problem lies with us (or a sinful world) rather than God. To complain therefore can be a reflection of a bad attitude that is, for example, not willing to accept responsibility or to accept God's will. Knowing that God does not approve of murmuring (Phil 2:14) or speaking evil of a brother (Jas 4:11), and that we will give account of our words (Matt 12:37), Num 12 serves as a good reminder to avoid such speech. When we don't receive what we ask for in prayer it may seem as if God has not heard us (Ps 22:1); when we grumble and complain, he surely does.

December 8
Keeping Up Our Spirits

WE OFTEN SPEAK OF "keeping up our spirits," usually referring to our maintaining an optimistic attitude or outlook. While happiness is a fine goal, we usually pursue it by emphasizing the things that make us happy; that is, things based in the physical realm (such as humor, a pleasurable meal, etc.). While these things are not necessarily wrong, a proper mindset for the Christian means they first pursue a spiritual, rather than a physical, goal. For the Christian the goal for which we strive is that of nurturing a strong spiritual life by giving attention to such things as a knowledge of God's word and a diligent prayer life (1 Thess 5:17). Such an emphasis is the scriptural remedy to overcome things that might deflate our spirit such as discouragement (Josh 1:9), hardships in life (2 Cor 12:10) and evil treatment by others (Matt 5:10–12). We keep up our spirits by keeping up our spiritual life—which may or may not make us happy.

December 9
Humility and Anxiety

TRYING TO CONTROL EVERYTHING ourselves may bring a sense of power but may bring with it some anxieties. Peter taught, "Humble yourselves, therefore, under the mighty hand of God . . . casting all your anxieties on him, because he cares for you" (1 Pet 5:6–7). To humble ourselves includes leaving our lives in God's hands, or turning ultimate control over to him. Since turning control over to anyone may bring with it anxieties, perhaps this is why Peter immediately tells us what to do with those fears. Before we can have the assurance of being able to cast anxieties upon God we need to humble ourselves before him. To do so brings the assurance that God has provided a way to overcome any fears that may arise. We may think we have life under control; but without humility before God, the fear may control us.

December 10

Re-Set Your Mind

WHEN WE SET SOMETHING on the table we expect it to stay there. Paul's command to "set your minds on things that are above" (Col 3:2) may make one think similarly regarding the mind. Being both a powerful and a flexible thing, the mind can affect one's life (Prov 23:7), and certainly their soul. For a good life, and to direct our soul toward heaven, the mind therefore must again be directed to think about the right things. Part of the definition of the Greek word translated "set" includes "keep thinking about," as if our mind will not stay on the table even though we set it there. The opposite of this concept is in Phil 3:19, wherein the same word appears of those who live "with minds set on earthly things." These things tell us of the imperative to give heavenly things our constant mental attention. One of the best ways to do this is to keep Jesus and his word, the bread of heaven (John 6:33), in our head (Deut 6:6–9).

December 11

"Let My Prayer"

THE PSALMIST RECOGNIZED THAT his worship is a spiritual, rather than a physical, activity: "May my prayer be established as incense before you, the lifting of my hands as the evening grain offering!" (Ps 141:2). When Christians worship God today through prayers, the Lord's Supper, preaching, giving, and singing, three of these avenues are intangible. In all of them our emphasis when we worship should be on the two spiritual aspects of "spirit and truth" (John 4:24). To do so can help us to keep our focus on the God who is a spirit, and help us avoid incorporating other activities (such as things that are more entertainment-oriented). This is not to say that concentrating on the spiritual can turn any physical activity (such as jogging) into a proper act of worship. Only that when we as Christians engage in the worship activities God has prescribed with the proper spirit and a proper life (1 Tim 2:8), and by treating worship as a spiritual exercise, can we thereby glorify God and be brought closer to him. Physical sacrifices in OT times may or may not have pleased God (Amos 5:21). The "spiritual" exercises of worship today may please him, but only if we treat them spiritually.

December 12

Blessed with Work

IT HAS BEEN OBSERVED that many of the things in our modern world, such as email, make our lives busier rather than provide us with more free time. The first appearance in the Bible of the word "blessed" is Gen 1:22, where God blessed animals he had created: "And God blessed them as follows: 'Be fruitful, and increase, and fill the waters in the seas; and let the birds multiply in the earth.'" We notice that this verse contains three commands, "be fruitful," "increase," and "fill." Is it a coincidence that this "threefold cord" is preceded by the word "blessed"? Just as the lights in the heavens are given the job of ruling over the earth (Gen 1:17–18), and humans are given work to do both before (2:15) and after the fall (3:17–19), so it is good for us to have work to do. Jesus said that he has work to do (John 9:4) and that his followers have work to do (John 4:35), about which we are to be constantly engaged (1 Cor 15:58). Simply keeping active for the sake of keeping active may not be a good thing; that is, to be busy with a purpose is surely the ideal. Yet it is also surely not good for the soul to be inactive or lazy (Prov 6:6–8); and while works do not save our soul, neither does doing nothing (Jas 2:24–26).

December 13
Overcoming Fear Part 1

SINCE FEAR IS THE opposite of faith (Rev 21:8), the Christian has a need to overcome fear. Fear is also crippling, even for those without faith. Three verses from the psalms help us to know what to do with this destructive emotion. One can plan on how to overcome fear in the event that very frightening circumstances arise. Psalm 23:4 again reads, "Even though I should walk through the valley of the shadow of death." The psalmist is contemplating a very scary situation (the deepest, darkest valley), which suggests he is presently not in that situation. While it is not good to spend one's waking hours contemplating the negative (Phil 4:8), one can nevertheless imagine, for comparative purposes, the worst that could happen, then use that picture to overcome the fear (as when saying "what's the worst that could happen"). Though perhaps a natural emotion, fear can be destructive to our soul. To imagine something fearful for the purpose of overcoming it can give us faith we might not have had otherwise.

December 14

Overcoming Fear Part 2

THE PSALMIST ELSEWHERE STATED his approach to fear in a way different from Ps 23:4: "When I am afraid, for my part I will trust in You" (Ps 56:3). Two noteworthy points from this verse include that, as in Ps 23:4 (see yesterday's "Daily"), he is again imagining the possibility of fear in the same way, only here in more general terms (as if to say "whenever I might be afraid"); he recognizes that fear is likely going to be a reality. The other point is that the word "I" in this verse is very emphatic (hence the translation "for my part," or it can also be translated "as for me"). While the reasons for this may be many, they could include the idea he will trust in God whether others do or not, and that overcoming fear boils down to one's own determination so to do. The child of God is blessed with the spiritual means to overcome this negative emotion, primarily that they have Someone (other than themselves) in whom they can put their trust.

December 15

Overcoming Fear Part 3

A THIRD WAY TO overcome fear is to heed the word of the Lord. Sometimes, like little children, we simply need to be told what to do. We certainly do not know what is best for us (Prov 14:12); and we may not realize the destructive nature of fear. Yet our Father does; so, as a father would say to his child "don't be afraid," God tells us to never be anxious (Phil 4:6). The psalmist expressed it "do not be afraid of the terror of the night, nor the arrow that flies by day" (Ps 91:5). The mention of night and day has a meaning of all of the time. The terror in the darkness, or something we cannot see, and the arrow of the day, something we can see, are not to be feared. This verse is not saying that these things cannot hurt us; but, not knowing whether these things will hurt us, we should avoid adopting an attitude that we know will hurt us. Rather than having a fear that will cause us to sink (Matt 14:30), we should rather believe our Father who tells us "don't be afraid."

December 16

"The Place We Ought to Worship"

JESUS' CONVERSATION WITH THE Samaritan woman in John 4 teaches many things regarding worship, including that children of God today are not limited to a specific location in order to worship God properly. She said to Jesus that the Jews say that Jerusalem is the place to worship (v. 20), to which Jesus replied, "Woman, believe me, the hour is coming when neither on this mountain nor in Jerusalem will you worship the Father" (John 4:21). The word "place" is often used in the OT with regard to a holy physical location (Exod 3:5; Deut 12:21). Today the "place" is spoken of as important for Christians (1 Cor 1:2; 1 Thess 1:8), yet it is not the physical, but the spiritual, that is, the holy actions in which Christians, engage that make the place special. Paul said, "I desire then that in every place the men should pray, lifting holy hands without anger or quarreling" (1 Tim 2:8). The place doesn't make us holy, but by gathering together to worship God the place is, as it were, special before God because of what we do there, our offering to him acts of worship from a life of holiness.

December 17

"He Thinks He Is Something"

TO BE IGNORANT OF certain things, such as the behavior of fire, can be dangerous to our well-being. To deceive ourselves, or to think we are right when we are not, is detrimental to our soul. Thus the Bible warns us of both ignorance and of self-deception (see, for example, such verses as 1 Cor 10:12, "Therefore let anyone who thinks that he stands take heed lest he fall"; Matt 7:22, "Lord, LORD, did we not . . ."; and Gal 6:3, "For if anyone thinks he is something, when he is nothing, he deceives himself"). Like all deception, self-deception is not based on truth, causes one to not know right from wrong (Mal 3:18), and does not excuse one before God today (Matt 7:23). The answer to ignorance is knowledge; one of the keys to acquiring knowledge is the knowledge that we are ignorant, which can then impel us to learn the truth. Otherwise we are playing with fire.

December 18

"Wearied the Lord with Words"

WORDS CAN BE DELIGHTFUL, as when one uses the right word to convey a tender emotion such as love; or words can be wearisome, as when one's ears are tired of listening to a conversation in which they are perhaps not interested. God has conveyed his will to man by means of his word (John 17:17), which does not change (Matt 24:35) nor "come to nought" (Rom 9:6). God does not tire of our words (Isa 59:1), unless we weary him with superfluous words (Matt 6:7), or words that convey false ideas. Malachi 2:17a reads: "You have wearied the LORD with your words. But you say, 'How have we wearied (him)?' When you say, 'Everyone who does evil is good in the eyes of the LORD, and he delights in them.'" What makes words important is the meaning to which they are tagged. What makes them wearisome is when they are used for such things as claiming evil to be good and good evil, as in Malachi. This passage also suggests that God is trying to hear them. If we use the right words, that is, words of truth, God will never tire of listening to us. With regard to our hearing God, it is not necessarily a love of words that keeps our ears directed toward God (2 Tim 4:4), but a love for truth, and thus the words used to convey that truth.

December 19

God's Harvest

JUSTICE IS A VALUED concept, especially when it goes in our favor. Christians are taught to think on the things that are just (Phil 4:8). We are often outraged when we see a person commit a crime for which they do not suffer any consequences, or when we ourselves try to do the right thing and seemingly receive no positive benefits. In like manner, God wearies of those who do not live right yet call out to him for justice (Mal 2:17). Yet God's harvest time is coming (Rev 14:15–16), though the ultimate court date is not during this life. In the meantime we must therefore believe God's promises of justice, to the point that even though injustice or evil seems to be alive and well, it will not survive God's harvest (Matt 3:12).

December 20

God's Response

OFTEN IN THE BIBLE a verse can again have a meaning of "do this . . . so that." When such verses include a response from God, they are not telling us what God needs, but what man needs. This is because God doesn't need anything, especially from us (Ps 50:12). So Mal 3:7b reads, "'Return to me, so that I may return to you,' is the pronouncement of the LORD of Hosts." Given the many verses that speak of God waiting for his wayward children to return (Isa 65:2), of his not changing (Mal 3:6), and of his perfection (Ps 18:30), this verse reminds us that God is, as it were, waiting for us to take the initiative in coming back to him. God didn't leave us, rather man left him. Whatever response (Jer 33:3), power (Eph 3:20), or beneficence (Luke 6:38) we desire from God depends on our initiative in asking God for his help. Malachi 3:7 tells us that, if we do, he certainly will respond. God does not need to return, but he will return if we will.

December 21

"With All My Heart"

JUST AS JESUS TAUGHT of our need to be wholly devoted to the Lord (Matt 22:37), so the psalmist similarly said, "Let me praise You with all of my heart" (Ps 138:1a). This statement by the psalmist suggests that it is possible not to worship God with all of our heart, and that to praise God with all of our heart therefore requires effort. This is also surely a matter between the worshiper and God; yet, perhaps some keys to carrying this out today would include thinking about every aspect of worship (that is, think about the words being sung, the words of the sermon, etc.). The avenues of worship in which Christians engage begin in the mind, and seemingly are both a reflection of and affect the heart. To praise God with all of our heart also suggests that none of our heart is left for ourselves, one ultimate purpose of which can be to avoid our worship being in vain (Matt 15:9) or being directed toward ourselves (Col 2:23). If we engage in worship with all of our heart we can then perhaps leave worship better equipped to do spiritual battle with worldly things (Eph 6:10–17), better equipped with a heart made stronger and closer to God because we have spent a brief hour praising him with all of it.

December 22

Light Within and Without

DURING THE TIME OF year when there is the least amount of light, Christians are reminded that there is a light within them. Jesus stated that "your eye is the lamp of your body. When your eye is healthy, your whole body is full of light, but when it is bad, your body is full of darkness" (Luke 11:34). Sometimes another source of light is needed to dispel the darkness (such as a runner might need when running in the pre-dawn darkness). God created the light that dispels darkness (Gen 1:3), and darkness did not overcome the light sent by God (John 1:5). The source of light for Christians is reflected in Scripture in such things as Jesus himself (John 8:12), the word of God (Phil 2:16). To overcome darkness Christians have a need to "be careful lest the light in you be darkness" (Luke 11:35), and to let this light shine (Matt 5:16; Phil 2:15), as well as to walk carefully in the light provided (1 John 1:7–9). God does his part in providing a light in which we are to walk; our need is to keep the light in us burning, in order to dispel the darkness around us.

December 23
"None Dies to Himself"

REALITY (HEB 9:27), COMBINED with the accumulation of years (2 Tim 4:7–8), can cause one to contemplate the inevitable moment of their death. Though perhaps unpleasant, as with many other aspects of life, death can be looked at from a physical or a spiritual perspective. Physically speaking, we naturally want our hour of death to be with little pain, a full heart, etc.; the spiritual perspective can include a desire for our departure to have an impact for good on those we leave behind. While death is the one journey we must make alone, Paul nevertheless said, "For none of us lives to himself, and none of us dies to himself" (Rom 14:7). Not dying to oneself suggests that, as Christians, we will leave some kind of spiritual legacy. It could be that our moment of death could have a greater spiritual impact than our life. If so, even though we won't be here to see it, we can use the time that we do have to heighten that impact (Eph 5:16). Whether the finish line is in view or a long way off (something we can't know for certain), we can reach for it, knowing that others have gone before and are cheering us on (Heb 12:1), that Jesus is waiting for us on the other side (John 14:2; Heb 12:2), and that we will leave others behind to possibly follow. If we run this race steadily in view thereof, it may be that our footprints will serve as an encouragement for others to follow, so that after that inevitable moment has come and gone, we can cheer them on toward the same goal and congratulate them when they win the race.

December 24

"These Were More Noble"

IN MANY COUNTRIES ONE either is or is not born into an upper position in society. To have a "high standing" in society is not necessarily wrong though, like riches, a danger of wealth and prestige is the possible corruption it can have upon the heart (1 Tim 6:17). Acts 17:11 describes the Jews of Berea as being "more noble" than those in Thessalonica: "Now these Jews were more noble than those in Thessalonica; they received the word with all eagerness, examining the Scriptures daily to see if these things were so." The Greek word translated "noble" has a meaning in other verses of someone in upper society, like a "nobleman" in old English society. Yet here the meaning has to do not with their social standing, but with their character. Their nobility is reflected in their actions with regard to God's word; that is, they received the word with an open mind, and examined the Scriptures daily to verify what they had heard. One may or may not, depending on whether they live in a democracy with free trade, be able to change their standing in life. More importantly, the word of God "is not bound" (2 Tim 2:9) unless it lands upon a heart that is closed (Acts 17:32). To be open-minded is necessary for one's initial conversion; to verify what one hears is necessary to ensure both receipt of truth and one's remaining on the path of light (1 John 1:7–9). Neither of these is a natural talent (that is, we can choose to have both). We can choose to be noble.

December 25

"Thanks Be to God"

How would we describe a gift? How a gift strikes us partly depends on us (our attitude). An extraordinary gift naturally will likely affect our soul to a greater degree; yet, what we do with this news still depends on us, including the extent to which we appreciated the gift. The Bible speaks of several gifts from God, including his son (John 3:16), the gift of the Holy Spirit (Acts 2:38), the gift of passing along the Holy Spirit (which was limited to the time of the apostles, Acts 8:20), etc. The reactions, such as those who praised God to the extent that it impressed others (Luke 1:17, 20), shows how gifts can affect the soul, and in turn bring glory to him. Some gifts, like a leper being given his health (Luke 17:11–19), are so beyond compare that the most we can do is to thank him (the fact that only one returned to do so, though, again illustrates that our response is up to us). Any gift from God can affect us for good. How would we describe a gift from God? Sometimes the most we can do is to say, "Thank you." "Thanks be to God for his unspeakable gift" (2 Cor 9:15).

December 26

Desire and Delight

DESIRE CAN BE BOTH a positive as well as negative drive, depending on the condition of one's heart. One danger of desire is that of harboring a heart that is constantly unsatisfied or, if the desire is misplaced, of the fulfillment thereof not being satisfying. While desires are natural, if we focus our delight on spiritual things, it can help satisfy our physical existence by leaving the fulfilling of desire up to God. Again, the psalmist said: "And take pleasure in the LORD, so that he would give you your heartfelt requests" (Ps 37:4). Desire can be redirected toward the Lord (spiritual) versus being directed only toward the physical. To do this can help one be "content with what you have" (Heb 13:5) rather than always wanting more. Whatever the nature of the desire, the answer is spiritual, that is, to delight in the Lord.

December 27

Glorify God First

To RECEIVE A GIFT or a reply to a request brings a type of glory to the recipient, in the form of the joy we feel upon receipt. God certainly wants us to pray (1 Thess 5:17), including for the purpose of submitting our requests (Heb 4:16). Again, our wants and desires can be a good thing (including serving as the motivation to pray), though simply getting what we want may not (Jas 4:3). Before teaching that we should "seek first the kingdom of God" (Matt 6:33), Jesus taught that the first element of our prayers should be words of praise to God, or "hallowed be your name" (Matt 6:9), after which we can make our requests (vv. 7–12). Before we ask for ourselves, it is good to offer something to God first. For a good relationship with God, we should offer him glory before expecting any for ourselves.

December 28

"Where Is My Honor?"

ONE OF THE PROBLEMS addressed by Malachi was that Israel had gotten careless in their worship (1:6–8). One can keep worship fresh if it comes from the heart (Ps 138:1). Even the most thrilling event, such as exciting entertainment, will become boring after repeated experience. In Mal 1:6 God asked, "A son is to honor (his) father, and a servant his master. So if am a father, where is my honor? And if I am a master, where is my fear? says the LORD of hosts to you, O priests, who despise my name. But you would say, 'How have we despised your name?'" By asking "where is my honor?" God is rebuking the nation through the priests for offering substandard worship. The Hebrew word translated "honor" has to do with bringing glory to God, but can elsewhere have to do with money, which Israel was also withholding (3:8). Giving our money is but one expression of our love for God. This is not because of the money—we can give it away with no heart being involved—but because of what it means, that we are willing to part with substance that helps us sustain our lives (Mark 12:41–44). To do so reflects that we are willing, perhaps among other things, to forego physical comforts in order to bring glory to God. The money, and therefore the honor, belongs to God (Hag 2:8). It should be a given that the father or master is to be given honor (Eph 6:2). God should never have to ask where is his.

December 29

No Way Out?

Problems in life usually cause us to look either for a resolution thereto, for the problem to just go away, or for a way of escape. It seems that when we look for answers to problems we naturally look to the physical realm (the Greeks of Paul's day believed that the body was the prison-house of the soul). During times of distress, pain, or such seeming entrapments as a bad marriage, one can feel as if there is no way for their soul to be free of their troubles. God provides a way out of temptation or testing (1 Cor 10:13). Satan promises freedom through sin, but, as with most forms of evil, the promise of freedom is actually a prison of sin (John 8:34). The answer to the longing of our soul to be free is not in such physical forms as "free" money, pleasure, or other physical distractions, but rather is spiritual. There is a way out; that way is the spiritual way of the One who said, "I am the way" (John 14:6).

December 30

What Are We Left With?

BOTH FUN TIMES AND hard times are going to come to an end. Both can have an impact on the soul, in that fun times can provide memories, while distress can leave one traumatized. This illustrates not only the temporary nature of events, but also the enduring nature of the spiritual effect of these things. The wise man said, "Even in laughter the heart can be in pain; and the result thereof is gladness (and) grief" (Prov 14:13). God would not have us to be Epicurean pleasure-seekers (1 Tim 5:6;), nor non-pleasure seeking Stoics (Acts 17:18), nor to wallow in such negative attitudes as worry (1 Pet 5:7) or anger (Eph 4:26). Rather, by concentrating on such spiritual things as God's word, God's will, and heaven to come, one can thereby become spiritually stronger (2 Cor 4:16) and be left with something that will endure. Just as we commemorate the changing of the year, one day the former things will have passed away, and God will wipe away any tears caused thereby (Rev 21:4).

December 31

"You Have Crowned the Year of Your Bounty"

THE PSALMIST IN Ps 65 praised God by observing the bounty that accompanied the end of the year: "You have crowned the year of your bounty" (v. 11a). One reason he could say this is because the Jewish New Year is in September, thus at harvest time. The psalmist praises God for the bounty of an abundant land, which is to be attributed to the way God cares for the earth (vv. 9–13). Is one to praise God only when there is an abundant harvest? Can a "bad" year be crowned with God's goodness? For the Christian, being able to praise God should not depend on how much substance we have (as Satan charged of Job 1:9–10). God is to be praised regardless, and God's goodness can be observed in other ways, such as all things working together for good (Rom 8:28). Like Habakkuk (3:17–18) we can, with a proper spiritual perspective, praise God whether we have abundance or not, and whether we can see any "good" or not. The present year is about to come to an end. God knew last year what this year was going to contain. We can know at year's end that everything, "good or bad," can work together for good—and thus praise God accordingly.

Afterword

THANK YOU FOR SHARING these biblical thoughts with me. It is my sincerest hope that, by pondering God's word on a regular basis, we may thereby grow spiritually by growing closer to him. The purpose of this book again was to help us be consistent in our spiritual outlook and approach to life.

On the one hand, writing is an expression of the thoughts (personality, soul) of the writer. On the other, there is a belief that once a writer's work leaves himself and enters the public arena it becomes more a part of the reader than of the writer. The material we have shared ultimately derives from God's word, the Bible. While we are therefore reading the thoughts of Dave, and possibly making them to some degree our own, our ultimate goal is that the thoughts that shape our heart and mind is God's word, the truth (John 17:17). We can know a lot about how life works, what makes it work, and what we can do in a practical way to facilitate life functioning. Yet it is the spiritual basis, or following the truth, by which the Christian can know that, no matter what physical events, problems, or joys befall them, these things are transient. And while they may impact our soul, they will pass. That with which we are left as we proceed through this life is the one thing that will last, the truth. The answer is spiritual.

Index

OLD TESTAMENT

Genesis
1:1	54
1:3	300, 357
1:10	112
1:17–18	347
1:22	347
1:31	226, 333
2:3	114
2–3	174
2:15	253, 347
2:16–17	47
2:18	54, 122
3:11	94
3:12–13	236
3:17–19	347
8:1	89
10:9	275
18:25	145
22:5	260
27:19	23
37:32–34	174
50:20	13

Exodus
3:5	351
12:14	251
14:13	321
14:27	321
15:1	317
20:2	261
20:7	115
20:8–10	114

Numbers
11:5	186
12	342
12:2	342
32:23	333

Deuteronomy
4:7	136, 330
5:15	251, 264
6	318
6:4–9	293
6:5	318
6:6	318
6:6–7	178
6:6–9	197, 211, 245, 345
6:7	318
7:7–8	93
12:21	351
15:15	153

Joshua
1	98
1:2	98
1:3	98
1:5	9
1:8	100
1:9	343
1:13	99

Joshua (cont.)

1:13 ESV	98
6:1	321
6:2	32

Judges

7:21	203

Ruth

1:16–17	195

1 Samuel

2:1	250
2:12	149
2:20	269
3:19	58, 307
3:20	54
16:7	261, 315

2 Samuel

12:13	236

1 Kings

8:27	301
17:13	4
18:20–29	238
18:27	342

1 Chronicles

	5

2 Chronicles

	5

Ezra

7:10	65, 66, 67, 329
7:12	65

Nehemiah

2:4	26
8:1	113
8:5	113

Job

1:9–10	366
1:21	127, 222
21:15	148, 149

Psalms

1	8, 24, 199
1:1	8
1:1–2	41, 112
1:1–3	267
1:2	96, 137, 293
1:3	64, 137, 199, 256
2:2–3	78
2:4	78
4:8	134, 254
5:3	90
8:1	115
9:1–2	131
13:6	91
18:30	355
19:1	120
19:7	140
19:14	69, 296
22:1	342
23:4	14, 70, 125, 143, 232, 273, 289, 326, 335, 348, 349
24:3–4	173
24:4	96
25:1	96
27:3	125
30:6	127
33:1	106, 317
34	171
34:3	126
34:14	34
35:19	156
37:1	43
37:1–10	43
37:4	33, 76, 96, 123, 146, 217, 241, 330, 361
37:5	144
37:6	43
37:7	43
37:8	43
40:3	317

46:1	185
50	341
50:8	341
50:9–11	341
50:10–13	281
50:12	168, 271, 355
50:12–13	260, 341
51:10	227
51:17	275
54:4	122
55	136
55:1	136
55:22	144
56:3	184, 349
56:3–4	211
61:1	342
61:4	185
65	366
65:9–13	339, 366
65:11a	366
67:4	145
91:1–6	185
91:5	143, 350
96:1	317
96:9a ESV	315
99	208
99:3	208
99:5	208
99:9	208
100:1	203
101	150
101:1	150
101:2–4	150
101:3b	150
101:4	150
101:5	150
101:7	150
101:8	150
103:1	74, 155
115:1	233
115:5	262
119:9	293
119:11	121
119:50	97
119:71	85
119:105	79, 273
119:114	185
121:1	12
122	163
122:1	163
122:2	163
122:6–8	163
122:9	163
127:1	164
133:1	195, 324
134	213
136:1	271, 281
137:4	250
138:1	363
138:1a	356
139:8	54
141:2	346
145:1–6	255
145:2	255
145:21	255
146	218
146:2	218
146:3	218
146:5	218
146:6	218
146:6–7	218
146:7–9	218
146:10	218
146–50	101
147:1	106
148:5	101
148:13	101
149:2	271
150:2	180

Proverbs

	322
3:5	57, 59
3:5–6	3, 60, 79
3:6	60
3:9–10	322
3:34	257
4:16	178
4:23	227
6:6–8	347
6:16–19	195
6:17	275
14:12	142, 350

Proverbs (cont.)

14:13	365
14:28	315
14:34	324
15:1	194
17:3	236
18:12	162
21:5	299
21:31	164
22:3	236
23:7	345
26:11	236

Ecclesiastes

4:12	80, 294

Isaiah

1:18	94, 263
5:20	55, 112, 158, 202, 319
5:24	319
18:5	91
21:6	90
26:3	1, 9
40:31	18, 52, 254, 267
41	205
41:20	205
55:8–9	142
55:11	58, 325
59:1	136, 342
59:2	130
59:15	226
61:1	223
61:2	223
61:3	223, 337
61:4	223

Jeremiah

6:14	263
8:20	266
14:12	238
20:9	329
31:34	312
33:3	76, 144, 241, 355

Lamentations

3:21	249

Ezekiel

12:2	262
20:46	307, 325
34:26	70

Daniel

1:8	14, 24, 335
3:17–18	289
3:18	133
8:12	307, 325

Hosea

4:1	312
4:6	88

Joel

2:21	321
2:24–27	321

Amos

5:21	173, 265, 336, 346
5:24	336
7:10	325
7:16	325

Jonah

1:2	23

Micah

7:8b	335

Habakkuk

1:2–4	159
1:5	159
3:17–18	143, 266, 366

Haggai

2:8	341, 363

Malachi

1:6	363
1:6–8	363
1:8	238, 275
2:17	354
2:17a	353
3:3	277, 309
3:6	355
3:7	355
3:7b	355
3:8	363
3:18	352

NEW TESTAMENT

Matthew

3:12	354
4	338
4:1–10	303
4:1–11	248
4:4	97
4:7	211
4:11	303
4:16	300, 307
5–7	74
5:9	81
5:10–12	343
5:16	300, 357
5:21–22	244
5:23–24	311, 336
5:27–28	244
5:43	156
5:43–44	244
5:44	176
5:45	143, 331
6:1	300
6:2	300
6:7	353
6:7–12	362
6:9	83, 362
6:9 ASV	115
6:10	71
6:11	102, 182, 212
6:19–20	181
6:20	102
6:21	127
6:22–23	227
6:24	155
6:25–33	259
6:25–34	256
6:26	111, 278
6:28	111
6:31–34	278
6:32	36
6:33	92, 116, 204, 297, 328, 341, 362
6:33 ASV	204
6:33–34	90
6:33a	239
6:33b	239
6:34	177, 182, 298
7:7	48, 168, 328
7:8	132
7:11	154, 331
7:16	112
7:20	219
7:20 ASV	170
7:21	115, 172
7:22	352
7:23	261, 268, 352
8:23–27	84
10:28	86, 189, 273, 285
10:33	128
12:4	283
12:7	172
12:37	342
13:31	304
13:44	65
14:28	179
14:28–30	118
14:30	4, 350
15:7	228
15:8 ASV	213
15:8–9	191, 238
15:9	113, 306, 356
16:18	35
17:5	234
17:10	234
17:20	214, 333, 337, 338
18:20	126, 286
21:28–31	167
22:37	356
23:12	193

Matthew (cont.)

24:35	160, 200, 216, 353
24:36	282
25:14–30	242, 284
25:23	284
25:29	284
25:41	228
26:30	250
26:39	32
26:39 ASV	190
26:41	239
26:42	71, 179, 257, 287
26:42 ASV	190
27:46	211
28:18–20	17, 221, 334
28:18–21	198
523–24	173

Mark

2:2	305
4:32	337
6:31	253, 254
6:41	304
9:1	216
11:12–14	242, 266
11:24	32, 70, 98, 183, 217, 232, 321
12:30	254
12:33	225
12:41–44	180, 275, 363
14:36	123
14:54	24
14:71	24

Luke

1:17	360
1:20	360
4:18–19	223
5:4–7	117
5:8	117
6:24	279
6:26	128, 277
6:33	133
6:35	331
6:38	141, 142, 144, 241, 244, 306, 311, 322
6:45	160
8	183
8:11	64
8:15	175
8:18	157, 174, 262
8:25	84, 183
9:23	282
11:10–13	241
11:34	357
11:35	357
12:15	182, 261
12:21	102
12:29 ASV	7
13:3	20
13:24	39
14:11	50, 162, 257
14:26	239, 268
14:28	164
14:28–30	37
15:17	174
15:18	23
15:20	23, 330
15:23	39
15:24	39
15:25–30	148
16:25	153
17:5	229
17:11–19	360
17:16	330
17:32	153
18	165, 230
18:1	11, 230, 269, 270
18:1–8	36, 179
18:5	165, 230, 269
18:8	183, 230
18:9–14	208
18:31	243
19:35	105
20:20 ASV	58
22:42	158, 164, 204, 232
23:46	304
24:8	89

John

1:5	357
1:14	216

1:29	237	9:2	63
2:22	121	9:3	63
3:12	111	9:4	347
3:16	93, 148, 268, 360	9:34	168
3:20	54	9:35	168
3:30	208	9:38	168
4	351	10:17	170
4:10–14	221	10:18 ASV	170
4:20	351	10:28	285, 309
4:21	351	10:29	189, 289
4:23	168	12:43	128, 234, 300
4:24	56, 155, 191, 221, 233, 265, 301, 332, 346	13	207
		13:17	66, 263
		13:19	187, 207, 288
4:32–34	221	14:2	228, 358
4:35	201, 347	14:6	80, 219, 307, 364
5	132, 147	14:15	207, 219, 276, 287
5:17	159	14:16	274
5:33	147	14:27a	129
5:36	147	15:4	199
5:39	132, 147	15:14	170, 207
5:44	132	15:25	156
5:45	132	16:12	325
5:46–47	132	16:13	216, 274
6:1–14	212	16:24	69
6:11	212	16:32	221
6:12	212	16:32 ASV	221
6:26	138	16:33	247, 274
6:33	345	17	40
6:33–35	221	17:9	210
6:38	71	17:11	290
6:60–66	288	17:17	22, 45, 73, 132, 140, 172, 175, 280, 288, 312, 324, 353, 367
6:63	142		
6:68	320		
7:17	146	17:20	195
7:19	146	17:20–21	324
7:24	261	17:21	195
8:12	357	18:37 ASV	219
8:31–36	22	19:28	243
8:32	45, 169, 186, 192, 263, 276, 280, 305	19:36	243
		20:8–9	316
8:34	186, 192, 210, 364	20:9	243
8:37	305	20:29	288, 316
8:43	305	20:30	187
8:44	192	20:31	187
9	168	21:25	305

Acts

2:31	92
2:37	94, 174, 196, 262, 263
2:38	94, 274, 360
2:41	92
2:47	199, 286
5:29	128
5:33 ASV	196
7:51	262
7:57	307
8:20	360
8:26–27	23
8:27	260
8:39	82
9:20	267
9:22	267
9:27	274
9:29	267, 274
9:31	272, 273, 274
9:36	270
10:25–26	271
10:38	170
11:23 ASV	283
12:11	174
14:19	133
15:24	313
15:32	313
16:4	314
16:4 ASV	314
16:25	250
17:11	325, 359
17:16 ?	332
17:18	365
17:21	48, 146
17:23 ASV	332
17:25	287
17:27	301
17:27a	328
17:32	325, 359
18:3	329
18:5	329
20:32	49, 185, 225, 302, 304, 320, 323, 333
20:35	74, 154, 306
21:14	179
23:1	334
27:23	210, 261
27:25	10

Romans

1:15	14
1:16	31, 58, 87, 160, 175, 185, 196, 220, 248, 267, 288, 303, 313, 323
1:20	111, 120, 310
1:24–25	191
2:4	20, 117
2:23	107
4:18	224
4:20	267
5:1	81, 129, 272
5:4	25, 86
5:11	107
5:12	236
6:1–2	240
6:4	197
6:16	210
6:17	82, 167, 227, 287
8:2	235
8:5	95
8:24	224, 340
8:26	36, 122
8:28	13, 16, 143, 171, 235, 244, 256, 283, 321, 366
8:29	226, 292
8:35	188
8:37	188, 189, 247
9:6	353
9:13	268
10:10	227, 267, 338
10:13	115
10:14	94
10:17	184, 195, 205, 227, 333, 340
11:6	240
12:1	282
12:1–2	245
12:2	103, 197, 226, 258, 270, 290, 292
12:2a	72

12:2b	72
12:8	320
12:9	152, 176
12:18	81, 171
12:20	244
12:21	34, 135, 152, 194, 201, 247, 285, 303, 333
13:1	78
14:7	358

1 Corinthians

1:2	351
2:9	159, 228
2:10	205
2:14	155, 244
3:2	325
3:8	266
3:10–15	35
3:14	75
4:1	322
4:2	242, 284, 341
6:7	194
6:9–10	47
6:11	47
6:19–20	212, 254, 341
6:20	210
9:22	128, 258
9:24	225
9:25	237
9:26	295
10:12	352
10:13	135, 248, 277, 309, 364
10:27	304
11:1	258
11:2	296
11:17–22	173
11:20	260
11:20–29	301
11:23	296
11:23–29	306, 330
11:24	153, 251, 327
11:25–26	327
11:27	275, 336
11:29	208
13:1	167
13:1–3	287
13:3	167
13:4	289
13:5	71, 123, 265, 276
13:5 ASV	103
13:6	93, 276
13:7	289
13:8	289
13:11	246
13:12	79
14:15	180, 203, 275, 291, 301, 306
14:37	296
15:3	296, 314
15:20	335
15:24	286
15:31	282
15:33	40, 258
15:55	247, 335
15:57	203
15:58	75, 104, 114, 148, 167, 201, 253, 288, 289, 347
16:2	131, 141, 180, 228, 265, 306, 311, 322

2 Corinthians

1:3–4	274
1:8	206
1:13	206
4:8	206
4:9	189
4:16	28, 42, 107, 189, 214, 225, 254, 267, 365
5:1	19
5:9	234
5:10	339
5:17	47, 197, 202
6:2	153, 298
8:2–3	141
9:6–11	141
9:7	203, 228, 265
9:10	239, 284
9:15	360

2 Corinthians (*cont.*)

11:14	192
11:23–27	279
12:7–10	323
12:9	44, 87, 107, 108, 109, 159, 216, 272, 302
12:9–10	236, 299
12:10	6, 84, 108, 109, 166, 177, 184, 257, 330, 343
12:10 ASV	229

Galatians

1:10	280
1:12	296
3:1	210
3:7	219
3:13	30
3:27	223, 246, 315
4:5	30
5:1	186
5:9	135, 148, 333
5:16	110
5:17	235
5:22	21, 129, 143, 170, 203, 209
5:22–23	56, 64, 209, 242, 266
5:25	221
6:2	122
6:3	352
6:7	266
6:14	282

Ephesians

1:3	272
1:7	29, 119, 175
1:12	66, 242
2:5	252
2:8–9	66, 130
2:8–10	301
2:10	270
2:12	130, 224
2:14	130
2:20	35
2:21	35
2:22	35
2:24	151
3:8	188
3:11–12	214
3:16	214
3:20	31, 220, 225, 302, 338, 355
4:1	37, 79, 295
4:15	93, 174, 194
4:18	227
4:25	246
4:26	43, 118, 365
4:29	53
4:30	308
4:31	43, 105, 118, 246
5:15	282
5:15–17	211
5:16	290, 298, 358
5:16 ASV	30
5:19	101, 228, 250, 286, 291
5:25	151
6:2	363
6:10	42, 135, 201, 258, 267
6:10–17	356
6:10–18	181, 308
6:10–20	181
6:11	81, 303
6:11–17	100
6:12	176
6:13	247
6:13–17	176, 177
6:16	285
6:17	97, 196
6:18	197

Philippians

1:23	329
2:3 RSV	162
2:5	7, 95, 103, 162
2:5 ASV	193
2:6–7	193
2:6–9	257
2:8	193

2:13	220
2:14	15, 342
2:15	300, 357
2:16	357
3:8	200
3:13	116, 153, 177, 264
3:13–14	27
3:14	124, 237
3:19	345
3:20	40, 290
4:6	118, 232, 331, 350
4:6 ASV	259
4:6–7	285, 321
4:7	38, 81, 129, 176, 285, 326
4:8	61, 62, 103, 139, 140, 152, 178, 245, 249, 264, 299, 339, 348, 354
4:9	129, 285
4:11	182, 279
4:11–12	127
4:12	6, 40
4:13	214, 215, 267
4:16	229
4:19	19, 77, 138, 176, 215, 340

Colossians

1:13	199, 286
1:29 ASV	220
2:6	82, 295
2:6–7	110, 199
2:7	82
2:12	199
2:23	332
2:23 ASV	158
2:33	356
3	97
3:2	2, 61, 97, 116, 177, 197, 227, 245, 345
3:5—4:6	97
3:9	246
3:10	246
3:16	113, 250, 291
3:17	75, 254, 284
3:21	245
3:23	57, 297
4:5 ASV	30

1 Thessalonians

1:3	224
1:8	351
2:9	279
2:10–13	315
2:11	51
4:1	37
4:13	224
4:13–18	249, 294
4:17	40
5:4–8	294
5:11	320
5:17	26, 83, 90, 197, 330, 343, 362
5:18	269, 331, 339

2 Thessalonians

1:7	253
2:12	263

1 Timothy

1:1	224
1:13	323
1:20	37, 289
2:1–2	163
2:1–4	83
2:1–8	228
2:8	113, 213, 346, 351
3:15	93, 163, 175, 307
4:8	18, 28, 67, 295
4:16	288
5:6	39, 96, 166, 365
5:8	297, 341
5:25	300
6:7	261
6:8	102, 212
6:10	24, 181
6:13	231
6:17	102, 359
6:18	34

2 Timothy

1:10	181
2:1	267
2:2	304, 314
2:9	359
2:12	21
3:7	67, 88, 161
3:12	277
4:2	211
4:3	263
4:3–4	73, 146, 192
4:4	48, 157, 262, 280, 307, 353
4:7–8	358

Titus

2:4	151

Philemon

	149

Hebrews

1:1–2	10
2:1	293
3:7	274
4:9	253
4:11	253
4:12	58, 216
4:16	15, 26, 76, 83, 136, 165, 179, 190, 230, 301, 323, 362
5:12–14	293
5:14	25, 28, 135, 205, 314
9:27	290, 358
10:24	320
11:1	183, 340
11:4	180
11:6	118, 230
11:16	186, 290
11:34	236
12:1	237, 246, 295, 358
12:1–2	264
12:2	209, 358
13:5	9, 68, 361
13:5–6	289
13:8	241
13:15	291

James

1:2	209
1:6–8	195
1:14	285
1:14–15	24
1:21	243, 293, 313
2:24	57
2:24–26	98, 347
2:26	231
3:5	160
3:6	171
4:3	83, 154, 165, 179, 321, 362
4:6	257
4:7	34, 135, 152, 248, 303, 333
4:8	96, 301
4:11	342
4:13–14	164
4:13–15	127, 217
4:14	116, 290
4:15	117, 164
4:17 ASV	152
5:13	180, 250, 317

1 Peter

1:3	19, 323
1:4	46, 243, 244
1:5	326
1:6	308, 326
1:7	309
1:8	330
1:13	14, 131, 294
1:14	226, 292
1:17 ASV	290
1:21	298
1:22	161, 172, 175, 200, 202, 219
1:23	216, 293
2:2	252
2:5	65
2:9	261

2:13–14	145
2:16	210, 251
2:19	334
2:21	237
3:7	324
3:7 ASV	151
3:10–11	171
4:4	290
4:11	113, 329
4:19	304
5:5	257
5:6	50, 142, 257
5:6–7	344
5:7	15, 105, 144, 259, 365
5:8	34, 81, 178, 201, 245, 258, 282, 285

2 Peter

1:5	318
1:6	318
1:8	318
1:12	318
1:14	246
3:9	305
3:16	205
3:18	xii, 22, 82, 161, 240, 252, 270, 318
3:18a	169

1 John

1:7	79, 266
1:7–9	173, 357, 359
2:3	16, 312
2:3–4	330
2:15	40, 268
2:21	169
3:2	142, 258
3:21	169
4:4	135
5:4	247
5:13	16, 266
5:14	70, 154, 217, 232
5:20	336

2 John

1:2	169

Jude

3	xii, 187, 325

Revelation

2:6	156
2:10	176, 188
2:10b	203
3:16	252
3:20	305
4:8	21
5:13–14	255
10:9	73
14:1	261
14:7	218
14:13	114, 254
14:15–16	354
19:8	246
19:10	155, 191, 260
19:10 ASV	271
20:4	99
21:1–4	340
21:4	39, 61, 166, 197, 273, 365
21:7	133
21:8	118, 125, 184, 192, 348
22:4	227
22:9	191
22:18–19	xii

www.ingramcontent.com/pod-product-compliance
Lightning Source LLC
Chambersburg PA
CBHW050834230426
43667CB00012B/1994